D1288217

Corsican Cuisine

THE HIPPOCRENE COOKBOOK LIBRARY

Corsican Cuisine

flavors of the perfumed isle

Arthur L. Meyer

Illustrations by John A. Wilson

Hippocrene Books, Inc.
New York

Color photographs by David H. Weber and Arthur L. Meyer.
Book and jacket design by Wanda España/Wee Design Group.

For more information, address:
HIPPOCRENE BOOKS, INC.
171 Madison Avenue
New York, NY 10016
www.hippocrenebooks.com

Library of Congress Cataloging-in-Publication Data

Meyer, Arthur L.
  Corsican cuisine : flavors of the Perfumed Isle / by Arthur L. Meyer ; illustrations by John A. Wilson.
       p. cm.
  Includes bibliographical references.
  ISBN-13: 978-0-7818-1248-1 (hardcover : alk. paper)
  ISBN-10: 0-7818-1248-8 (hardcover : alk. paper)
1. Cookery, French--Corsican style. 2. Cookery--France--Corsica. 3. Corsica (France)--Social life and customs. I. Title.
  TX719.2.C67M494 2010
  641.5944'99--dc22
                              2009046736

Printed in the United States of America.

 "Mette a casa in corpu!"

"Put the house in the body!" (Offer a warm welcome of food.)
—An old Corsican saying

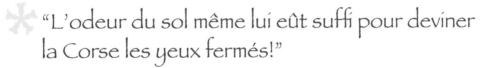 "L'odeur du sol même lui eût suffi pour deviner la Corse les yeux fermés!"

"The scent of the land alone is enough to recognize Corsica with eyes closed!"
—Attributed to Napoleon Bonaparte.

For Lena, my favorite kitchen assistant.

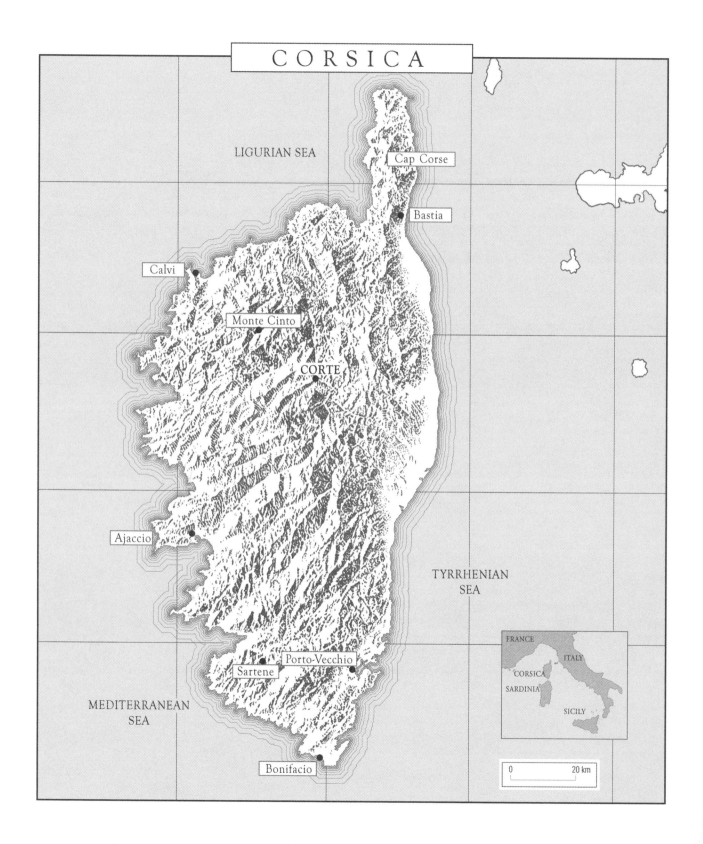

Contents

Preface

It is exciting to be able to write about a comparatively unknown cuisine. As with all cooking traditions, there are influences that mold them, but Corsican cooking uses flavorings unique to the island. Simple and without elaborate preparation, it is a cuisine that is familiar, yet mysterious, like the island and its people. The meat, game, and dairy are perfumed with the essence of wild herbs growing under mountain-cooled winds. Hams and other charcouterie, made from pigs that are free to graze on the wild herbs and then allowed to feed to their hearts' content on chestnuts from the fall harvest, are admired and desired by the most discerning gourmets. Cheeses made from ewe's and goat's milk are specialties not to be missed in Corsica. Also free to graze on myriad herbs and aromatic shrubs, lambs and goats, as well as the milk and dairy they provide, are redolent with the perfume of wild herbs known as the *maquis*.

Corsican recipes are easy to prepare and packed with flavor. The foundations of the cuisine are rich stews, hearty soups, and simply prepared fish and game. Pastas, polentas, and filled crêpes round out the customary dishes that define Corsican fare. But there are surprises everywhere. The polenta may be made with chestnut flour rather than cornmeal, and lasagna could be filled with a stew of rabbit, rather than tomato sauce and cheese. The haunting flavor of myrtle liqueur (*myrte*), a tradition of the island, may infuse a Corsican cheesecake.

More than the birthplace of Napoleon and the vendetta, Corsica is a culinary treasure that should not be overlooked by chefs, home cooks, restaurateurs, food writers, and everyone interested in flavorful, healthy, and simply prepared dishes.

Introduction

Imagine a cuisine with Italian influences but a distinctly different range of recipes. Its rustic breads, savory pastries, luscious tarts, and artisinal cheeses bring to mind the specialties of rural France. But here the cheeses, made from fresh ewes' and goats' milk, are instilled with the aromatic underbrush on which livestock are allowed to graze. Mediterranean influences abound as well. Exquisite in its simplicity, a sauce made from fruity olive oil, garlic, and parsley dresses a trout just caught in an icy-clear mountain stream, a Mediterranean-style dish with a Corsican twist—the trout are grilled on a heated stone over a wood fire.

The foods of Corsica make up a hearty cuisine that reflects its rugged and mountainous terrain. Mostly granite, Corsica is part of the Alps mountain range, jutting out majestically through the most beautiful azure water in all of the Mediterranean. The bounty of the sea adds to the rustic, amply flavored dishes of the island. The perfume from rolling fields of wild herbs infuses richness into all the foods of Corsica. When slowly roasted over coals, lamb releases aromas of wild thyme and Corsican mint. Spicy myrtle wood is often used when building a cooking fire to impart additional flavor. The fragrance of pork roasting over myrtle wood, from pigs free to graze on plump chestnuts is remarkable.

In some ways the Corsican approach to seasoning is similar to that of North Africa, India, and the Middle East. As these regions combine many spices together, Corsica blends its herbs, including wild thyme, myrtle, rosemary, bay laurel, wild mint, sage, fennel, nepita (calamint), marjoram, juniper, and chamomile. The bees also find Corsican herbs irresistible and produce honey in a broad spectrum of flavors, from a peppery, dark, and bold variety produced from stands of chestnut trees, to the silky, mellow sweetness of sage blossom honey.

To some it may seem puzzling that Corsica could be overlooked by food writers and chefs for so long. Several factors have contributed to this lack of exposure. Corsica has never been separated as an entity distinct from its ruling French and Italian governments; rather it has been relegated to small chapters or brief mention, if any, in their cookbooks. Also, the distinctiveness of its cuisine makes it an uneasy fit with Mediterranean, Italian, and French cookbooks. Thus it is rarely included in the anthologies that are often the starting points to solo books on the subject. Few travelers outside the immediate region of Corsica have access to the island. Its short summer tourist season is overwhelmed by regional French and Italian visitors. Intense nationalism and a mood toward preservation of remaining unspoiled territory discourage development that would accommodate additional tourism. Because of these factors there is little interest by Corsica to publicize their region as a destination for Americans and other English-speaking tourists.

As early as 550 BC the Ionian Greeks settled Corsica. The island was conquered by Rome in 259 BC, as part of the first Punic War. The fall of the Roman Empire brought occupation by the ancient Vandals of Germany, followed by the Byzantine

Empire, and then the Moors. By the eleventh century Corsica came under the influence of Pisa and its political and commercial rival, Genoa. Genoa achieved complete rule of Corsica by the fourteenth century and held onto that role until the eighteenth century. It would provide the most influence on the cuisine of Corsica. Situated just north of the island of Sardinia, the island of Corsica was given to the French in 1768, as a result of intervention by France and England, due to a series of revolts by the Corsicans led by the patriot Pasquale Paoli.

The cuisine of Corsica is distinctive. It has only a minor relationship to classical French cooking, in spite of being part of France since the mid-eighteenth century. There are some aspects of its use of herbs and seasonings that remind one of Provence, but it is not Provençal cooking. French baking traditions are more soundly linked to Corsican cooking. Italian influence should be much more significant, based on Corsica's history, yet similarities are not particularly strong. Corsicans are extremely nationalistic and throughout their history they have resisted outside influence on their culture. This has led to assimilation of only those aspects of cooking that fit into their unique style of food preparation and flavoring.

Corsican food is assertive, flavorful, and simply prepared. It is rich in wild herbs from the *maquis*. Corsica produces some of the finest *charcouterie* in the world. There is a "slaughter of the pig" festival celebrated annually at the Renno fair in February. Surrounded by the sea and with pristine mountain streams, Corsican seafood and fish are simply prepared in a manner that is unique, scented with Mediterranean accents. Grilled meats, such as lamb and kid goat, are prepared over open fires, basted with brushes made from wild herbs. Cattle are free to graze on lush pastures filled with these aromatics. In particular, myrtle and *nepita* (also known as Corsican marjoram, peppery mint, thyme basil, and calamint) are used extensively and impart a characteristic flavor that helps to define Corsican cuisine, as do wild mint and wild thyme. Southern Corsican recipes can contain traditional spices of North Africa, such as cinnamon, cardamom, and saffron. As is often the case, herbs and spices not used in a cuisine can also help to define it. Oregano, a common herb of Italy and most of the Mediterranean region, is rarely used.

Cornmeal is a staple commonly eaten in the form of *polenta* and *gnocchi*, as is chestnut flour, although chestnut flour has become expensive for daily consumption. Semolina pastas such as *ravioli* and *involuti* are popular. Rice dishes are prepared much like in neighboring Spain, slowly cooked and never stirred (the technique for cooking paella, the famous Valencia rice dish), and unlike the creamy risottos of Italy, which thrive on stirring to release starches.

Wild mushrooms, such as boletes (porcini) and girolles (chanterelles) are plentiful and delicious, and are considered regional delicacies. Olive and citrus groves have been successfully transplanted to the island and olive oil is most often used in cooking. Olives are also featured in some of Corsica's recipes. A ricotta-style fresh ewes' milk cheese, *brocciu*, is Corsica's most famous cheese. It is also available aged, as a firm, sharp, grating-style cheese.

While the untarnished waters surrounding Corsica are the envy of the Continent, the seas have been over-fished for centuries. But there is indication that, with careful management, the fishing industry is making a comeback. Day fishing is most common and the daily catch is primarily distributed locally. Popular seafood and fish include sardines, eels, cuttlefish, sea spiders (resembling long-legged lobsters or king crabs), sea urchins, squid, mullet, tuna, and trout. Clear mountain streams are an important source of fish for the family table. Interestingly though, Corsican

alvi is considered the cultural capital of Corsica. With expensive shops and restaurants along with multi-million-dollar yachts in its harbor, Calvi may remind you of the tony resort towns along the Côte d'Azur. Music festivals abound in Calvi and in mid-September the *Rencontres de Chants Polyphoniques* festival is held to celebrate Corsica's traditional music style, polyphony (many voices). The music is performed without instrumental accompaniment, *a cappella*, and like much of Corsica, the songs are haunting and mysterious. Since the 1970s there has been a resurgence of interest in all things Corsican and polyphony has thrived since. One specific form of polyphony defines Corsican music tradition. The *paghjella* is a short, two-minute song, often described as profane and sacred at once. It is sung by three voices (although *paghju* means pair in Corsican), with specific roles assigned to each singer. These ancient-sounding songs of torment and longing come from deep within the soul.

Calvi

cuisine does not rely heavily on fish and seafood. Historically the island's coast was known for its tall, straight pines, and was constantly raided for the trees, which made fine masts for sailing ships. To avoid hostilities, Corsicans moved into the mountainous terrain for protection. As well, the coastlines were mosquito-infested, breeding malaria, until Americans eradicated the problem during World War II. So in spite of being an island, Corsica's cuisine is clearly of the mountains and plains.

THE LAND AND PEOPLE OF CORSICA

THE COUNTRY

Corsica is an island in the Mediterranean, approximately 110 miles from north to south and 50 miles wide. Just ten miles separate it from Sardinia to the south, by the Strait of Bonifacio. It's about 100 miles south of continental France, of which Corsica is a possession. Corsica is considered a region of France, but enjoys a slightly elevated status from the twenty-five other regions. Being part of the Alps mountain range, the island has fifty summits higher than 6,500 feet and the tallest mountain on the island, Monte Cinto, is almost 9,000 feet. Because of this, temperatures can vary greatly depending on elevation. It is not uncommon for snow to be falling in the mountains while people bask in the sun at the seashore. With over six hundred miles of coastline, Corsica has more than two hundred scenic beaches.

The population is just over 275,000, making Corsica the least populous region of France. Almost half of these people live in Ajaccio, the regional and historic capital in the south, and Bastia, the unofficial business capital in the north. Most of the villages have less than one hundred residents.

THE LAND

Corsica's most famous son, Napoleon Bonaparte, claimed that he would recognize Corsica with his eyes closed from the scent alone. Over half of the surface of Corsica is covered with aromatic evergreen plants known in Corsican as *macchia* and in French as the *maquis*. Throughout history, the *maquis* has served as an impenetrable refuge for Corsicans fleeing attack by many nations. It is also the traditional hiding place of Corsicans who have committed revenge murder (*vendetta*), and was instrumental in hiding French partisans from the Nazis and Italians during World War II.

The aroma of the *maquis* represents the very soul of Corsica, as it perfumes the island and surrounding seas. The *maquis* is the result of centuries of over use and grazing of the oak forests. As the oaks and their undergrowth retreated, the landscape became dominated by an assortment of hearty plants, for which Corsicans have developed many uses. The *maquis* is at its most spectacular in the spring, when hillsides are covered with a panorama of flowers; these blooms are the source of Corsica's highly prized and aromatic honey. The root systems of the plants of the *maquis* hold precious soil during Corsica's torrential fall and winter rains.

The native herbs of the *maquis* are used in all aspects of Corsican cuisine. These include rosemary, thyme, sage, marjoram, nepita (calamint), assorted mints, fennel, lavender, wild onions, and garlic. In shady areas of the *maquis*, myrtle takes over. Its branches are used as skewers for grilling, and the wood is commonly used as an aromatic additive to cooking fires. The leaves, berries, and oil extracted from them are used as a flavoring in stews and soups, and in the famous Corsican liqueur known as *myrte*. The arbutus tree of the *maquis* produces fruits that are inedible when raw, but when cooked make a popular Corsican jelly (*gelée d'arbouses*). They are also used in desserts and for flavoring liqueurs.

Wild and domestic pigs, sheep, and goats graze on the plants of the *maquis* and the native acorns and chestnuts, imparting a wonderful flavor to the meats and *charcouterie* of Corsica. Shepherds who seek new grazing grounds for their stock are sometimes blamed for starting destructive wildfires that seasonally ravage the *maquis*. Careless travelers and lightning are likely causes as well. While it is not yet threatened with extinction, the *maquis* is hard-pressed to come back after fire and it is often replaced by a low growing and coarse growth known as the *garigue*.

THE PEOPLE

Traditions

Retaliation is an important tradition in Corsica. It is called *vendetta*. Should a family member be harmed by another, the nearest relative is obliged to seek revenge on the perpetrator or on one of their family members. In Corsica, time does not heal all wounds, for the vendetta must be carried out, regardless of passage of time. As you may imagine, retaliation is met by a responding retaliation, and on and on, generation after generation. Occasionally a mediator may be brought in to end the bloodshed, but this is rare.

One of the world's more mysterious cultural beliefs can be found on Corsica. It involves the *mazzeri*, or dream hunters, usually women who can portend death. In their dreams the *mazzeri* hunt and kill animals. When they look into the face of the animal about to be killed, they see the face of someone from the village that is going to die. Corsican mythology is filled with stories of humans assuming animal form. The dream hunter kills the animal and the next day tells of the dream, often foretelling that the person will die within a year, in an odd number of days from the prediction. *Mazzeri* have nothing to do with *vendetta* or political revenge. They do not believe that they cause the death; to them the death has already occurred. Popular belief holds that *mazzeri* have special psychic gifts and that they

The evil eye, *l'ochju* or *ghjettatura,* can be warded off by the hand signal of making horns with index and pinky finger extended or a clenched fist with thumb protruding between the index and middle fingers. While the evil eye can be cast by accident with no malice intended, it is a serious matter when it is given intentionally. To remove the curse one seeks out a *Signadore* to diagnose the problem. The *Signadore* is usually a woman who has been imparted abilities from her mother or grandmother on Christmas Eve. She is considered an exorcist. The ritual of diagnosis involves interpreting the conformation of warm olive oil poured over the surface of a soup plate of water. If the oil refuses to coalesce into one large drop, in spite of coaxing with the *Signadore's* finger, the evil eye is present. The evil eye can be given remotely using a lock of hair or photo and the *Signadore* can break the spell remotely by using a lock of hair as well.

were improperly baptized as children, the priest or godparents somehow omitting a word or gesture in the ceremony.

THE CORSICAN LANGUAGE

To many, conversations in Corsican sound very much like spoken Italian. Until about thirty years ago, Corsican was considered to be a dialect of Italian. The language is now understood to be a unique Romance language, with many of its Latin roots in common with Italian. However, about 40 percent of the lexicon is not of Romance origin. Corsican has been an oral language for most of its existence; only since the end of the nineteenth century has it been set down in written form. Because of this and the rugged terrain of the land (which fostered isolation of communities), many dialects are in use across this small island. To add to the confusion, there are often multiple spellings of the same Corsican word.

The official language of Corsica is French, as Corsica has been a part of France since the end of the eighteenth century. Public education treats Corsican as a subject, much like an elective music class. Many have never been exposed to Corsican as a formal language. Corsican is most likely to be spoken among family members and neighbors, and so Corsican is usually learned from family interaction. The Catholic Church is a French institution and very little Corsican is spoken during services. This may account for the overall lack of regular religious participation among Corsicans. (A 1998 survey estimated that only 8 percent of the population attended church regularly.)

The future is hopeful for the use of the Corsican language. The people are intensely nationalistic and want to preserve that which separates them from France. Road signs increasingly appear in both languages. The Corsican language is voluntarily being woven into the curriculum of primary schools and Corsican culture is being included more widely in all areas and levels of education.

FLAVORS AND INGREDIENTS THAT DEFINE CORSICAN CUISINE

MYRTLE

I know of no other people that takes advantage of myrtle as the Corsicans do. A defining ingredient of the cuisine, myrtle is used as an herb much like bay leaf or thyme. The berries are the basis for the famous Corsican liqueur and are used to flavor game. Myrtle wood adds spice to a fire and its branches work as skewers to roast meats over coals. True myrtle, *Myrtus communis*, is a shrub that grows to ten feet in height. Its aromatic leaves, with flavors reminiscent of eucalyptus and pine, are used in many of Corsica's rich soups and stews. The berries are used in making sweets such as jellies, confitures, liqueurs, and syrups. They are added to pâtés and often accompany game dishes in sauces.

Pliny the Elder mentions its use in ancient texts, especially the addition of myrtle berries to sauces for game. Early recipes from Genoa called for myrtle to flavor meats and game, but it is not often seen in Italian recipes today. There is a popular myrtle liqueur from Corsica's closest Italian neighbor, Sardinia, called *Mirto*. Mortadella, a large Italian sausage, has its name derived from the myrtle flavoring originally added. The name for myrtle in Corsican is *morta*. The wood makes a wonderful addition to a cooking fire, and it is also used to fabricate baskets, brooms, and fishing traps.

OLIVES, OLIVE OIL

Wild olive trees have been growing on the *maquis* for centuries, but cultivation for oil and table consumption came into full production only by the mid-eighteenth century. Most of Corsica is adaptable to olive tree cultivation, and local oils abound. Pork fat and lard are flavorful additions to a recipe, but olive oil is the basis of most cooking on the island. Olives are included in recipes, a culinary gift from Provence, whose cuisine has been an important influence on modern Corsican cooking.

NEPITA AND THE HERBS OF THE MAQUIS

Nepita, also known as calamint and basil thyme, is related to thyme and catnip. Along with myrtle, nepita is rarely encountered in the world's myriad cuisines. It is considered a medicinal herb in America, but is difficult to find. The Internet is an excellent source, as I ordered seeds online to grow a miniature *maquis* in my garden.

Mint is an herb often associated with North African and Middle Eastern cuisine and its influence on the cuisine of Corsica is felt most in the southern regions of the island, but wild mint is common to all regions.

Thyme is indispensable when reproducing the flavors of Corsican dishes. Saffron, lemon, and cloves, all flavors of lands to the south, filter into southern Corsican cooking as well. Fennel seed is prevalent in recipes, as is the bulb and fronds, for soups, stews, and vegetable dishes.

While less than enthusiastic for church attendance, Corsicans passionately celebrate religious festivals, Easter in particular. Many villages and towns will have processions on Good Friday, weaving among the streets in a planned spiral fashion. The spiral, *A Granitula*, is found everywhere in Corsica, from logos on packages to patterns on church walls. The spiral, seen in the conch shell, represents a continuum, with no beginning or end. It is also seen as representing the cycle of life and resurrection. The coiling and uncoiling of Easter processions represents all of these things and is also symbolic of darkness becoming light and winter becoming spring.

Granitula

BROCCIU

It is difficult to find a recipe for soup, salad, meat, game, fish, vegetable, or dessert that does not call for the famous cheese of the island. Brocciu is a cheese often made from equal amounts of ewe's milk and goat's milk. It comes fresh, like ricotta or cream cheese, and in varying degrees of age and dryness, the oldest being excellent for grating, similar to fine parmesan. Fresh brocciu is found in many pastries and cakes, including an excellent cheesecake, often flavored with Corsican myrtle liqueur that can be found everywhere. Buns and tarts are filled with sweetened brocciu, and are the mainstay of local bakeries.

CHESTNUTS

Chestnuts have been mentioned as early as the thirteenth century in literature, but pollen studies have indicated that the tree has been on Corsica since the Neolithic period. In the sixteenth century, Corsica was part of the Genoese city-state and in 1584 the governor of Genoa ordered all landowners to plant four trees—chestnut, olive, mulberry, and fig. By 1700, 70 percent of some regions of the island were covered with chestnut trees. Chestnut flour, and the fruit itself, was a staple of the diet. After World War I, the chestnut forests began to decline, due in part to the loss of many young men who were needed to tend to the orchards. Disease was another factor in the decline. Today, chestnut flour is quite expensive, even within Corsica; almost 100 percent of the chestnut harvest remains on Corsica for local consumption. Regardless, it is a very important ingredient in Corsican cuisine and two annual festivals attest to this. Preparations for the annual harvest begin in August and the harvest starts in early October and lasts through November. Chestnuts are harvested by hand, only after they fall from the tree. The Chestnut Blossom Festival in November and the *Fiera di a Castagna* held in December attest to the significant roll the chestnut plays in the economy and cuisine of Corsica. Chestnut flour is used to make breads, polenta, and many cakes and pastries. The fruit is used in savory dishes and is preserved and candied for sweets and pastries. Wild pigs graze on chestnuts and this imparts a flavor to the charcouterie that makes Corsican hams and sausages world renowned.

HONEY

Honey is enjoyed in many ways, from a simply prepared dessert of Corsican cheese drizzled with honey, to a bold-flavored cheesecake. Bees lead busy and fruitful lives in Corsica. From the fields of wild herbs of the *maquis*, to stands of proud chestnut trees, bees have a wide selection of pollen to harvest and uniquely flavored honeys to make. From the most delicate to strongest, Corsican honeys are placed into six categories. *Printemps* is delicate, fruity, and golden, and is produced in the valleys of fruit tree orchards and vegetable gardens of the spring. *Fleurs de maquis* is produced from the spring flowers of the wild herbs of the mountains. It has a floral bouquet and is amber in color. *Miellat du maquis* is dark, brooding, and has a long-lasting caramel finish that can be bitter (in a positive way). *Châtaigneraie* is dark amber and comes from chestnut orchards. Its flavor is uniquely floral and strong, with woodsy overtones and a long finish. *Été* is quite sweet and aromatic. It is a late-summer honey, primarily from thyme and geranium. *Automne-hiver*, as its name suggests, is a late-fall/early-winter honey and comes from the woody flora of the *maquis* in winter. It has a woodsy nose and the clear, amber liquid is quite thick.

CHARCOUTERIE

Charcouterie is the crowning jewel of Corsican specialties. Corsica's hams and sausages are known throughout Europe as being the finest, with delicate flavors imparted by pigs grazing on the wild herbs of the *maquis*, and being fattened with chestnuts from the fall harvest. All products are proudly made by hand; mechanization is shunned throughout the island.

Coppa is made from pork loin that has been salted and smoked for three to four weeks and then hung in caves to dry and age. *Ficatellu* is a sausage made from pork liver, lean meat, various organs, and blood and is seasoned with laurel, rosemary, garlic, and red wine. *Lonzu* is the loin of pork that has been salted and dried, and is coated with cracked pepper. *Lonzu* is also produced in Italy and in Spain where it is called *lomo*. *Panzetta* is a roll of lean bacon made from the breast of pork, and is known as *pancetta* in Italy. *Prisuttu* is the mountain air-dried and cave-cured ham of Corsica and is similar to Bayonne ham from the Basque region, *jamons* Serrano and Iberico from Spain, and prosciutto from Italy. *Salamu*, a dried salami, and *salcicetta*, a cured sausage, are both found in traditional Corsican dishes.

Recipes

There's an old saying in Corsica *"Ou mange la soupe ou . . . saute par la fenêtre"* which translates as "Eat your soup or … jump out the window." Corsicans are fanatical about their soup. If a villager wants to know if you have eaten dinner he asks, "Have you souped yet?" In the town of Morosaglia, a museum dedicated to Pasquale Paoli, the national hero of Corsica, boasts only four items—a statue, his sword, his ashes, and his soup tureen!

Soup is hearty fare, essential for hard-working people living in a rugged environment. Corsica is not the place to go to sample a delicate consommé. Its soups are thick, slowly simmered, and full of herbs that follow the seasons. Often soup is the meal, rather than a beginning to the meal, usually served with a fritter, a bit of cheese, and a fried egg. Often brimming with vegetables, legumes, and beans, you can also expect to find pasta, chickpeas, and potatoes in a soup. Peasant Soup will remind you of rich Italian minestrone, and the chestnut soup, thick with puréed chestnuts, may startle you with the tang of fresh goats' milk stirred in at the last minute.

SOUPS

Garlic Soup

SOUPE À L'AIL

MINESTRA INCU L'AGLIU

SERVES 4

A soup for all seasons, this is especially favored when the garlic is in full bloom but before it has sprouted (from May through July). The soup is surprisingly delicate, considering the amount of garlic used.

Advance Preparation: Separate the cloves of garlic and peel them. Crush the garlic cloves with the back of a knife, but do not chop them. Peel and dice the potatoes and place them in a bowl of water to prevent browning.

1. Fill a medium pot with 6 cups cold water and add the crushed garlic, potatoes, olive oil, bay leaf, and sage. Bring to a boil, and then turn down the heat. Simmer over low heat for 20 minutes.

2. Remove the garlic and herbs with a slotted spoon and reserve the garlic.

3. Beat the egg yolks with some of the hot stock to temper. Slowly add this mixture to the soup, whisking constantly. Lower the heat and allow the soup to thicken slightly, stirring constantly—but do not allow the liquid to boil, as it may scramble the eggs.

4. Adjust seasoning with salt and freshly ground pepper. Serve immediately, topping each soup bowl with a slice of toasted bread spread with the reserved garlic.

Notes: The reserved garlic may be puréed and stirred into the soup. The toast may be topped with a soft-boiled egg for a traditional method of serving. One-half cup of dry vermicelli noodles may be added 10 minutes before serving.

Ingredients

1 large head garlic, fresh and aromatic

2 medium new potatoes

2 tablespoons olive oil

1 small bay leaf, fresh if available

4 small fresh sage leaves

2 egg yolks

salt and freshly ground pepper to taste

4 thin slices toasted rustic bread

Red Bean and Leek Soup

Ingredients

2 cups small dried red beans

4 cups sliced leeks, white and light green parts only, thoroughly washed (about 5 leeks)

¼ cup olive oil

3 garlic cloves, minced

4 sprigs fresh thyme

1 fresh bay leaf, bruised with the back of a knife

1 tablespoon chopped fresh sage leaves

5 ounces cooked pork loin (smoked or not), finely diced (about 1 cup)

8 cups cold water or stock

salt and pepper to taste

assorted chopped fresh herbs for garnish (*optional*)

toasted rustic bread slices (*optional*)

SOUPE AUX POIREAUX ET AUX HARICOTS ROSES
MINESTRA DI FASGIOLU E DI PORRI

SERVES 6 TO 8

Dried beans are a staple of Corsican cooking and usually appear in soups and vegetable dishes. Leeks are also often used in Corsican cuisine, and this traditional soup is served in most villages.

Advance Preparation: Soak the beans in cold water to cover for 30 minutes. Drain the beans, discarding the soaking liquid.

1. In a large pot, sauté the leeks in olive oil over low heat until soft and just beginning to turn golden. Add the garlic and sauté 1 minute.
2. Toss in the thyme, bay leaf, and sage. Lower the heat and stir 1 minute. Add the pork loin.
3. Add the soaked beans and 8 cups water or stock. Raise the heat, bring just to a boil, and then lower the heat so the mixture is at a simmer.
4. Skim the surface of the liquid if necessary and partially cover the pot. Simmer 1 to 1½ hours over low heat, adding water as necessary.
5. Adjust seasoning with salt and pepper.
6. To serve, top the soup with chopped herbs and add a thick slice of toasted bread on the side.

Notes: Any dried bean will do for this recipe. Substituting stock for water adds flavor. Other fresh herbs may be added while cooking or as garnish. For a vegetarian version, omit the pork and add 1 cup diced zucchini. Purée a portion of the soup and stir it back in for more texture.

Chickpea Soup

MINESTRA INCU I CECI

SERVES 6 TO 8

This soup is traditionally served on Holy Thursday, the day before Good Friday, but is also served year-round. The full name of the soup is Chickpea Soup for Holy Thursday (*minestra incu i ceci di jovi santu* or *soupe de pois chiches du Jeudi saint*). For many in lean times, meat had to be replaced with dried legumes, and chickpeas were a nutritious substitute.

Advance Preparation: Soak the dried chickpeas in cold water to cover for 30 minutes. Drain and rinse.

1. In a medium pot, add the soaked chickpeas to 6 cups cold water and heat to boiling. Lower the heat and bring to a slow simmer. Simmer 2 to 2½ hours, until the chickpeas are tender, adding water as necessary.
2. Add the minced garlic and olive oil to the simmering chickpeas. Cook 10 minutes.
3. About 10 minutes before serving, toss in the pasta and continue to simmer the soup until the pasta is cooked.
4. Serve with grated cheese.

Notes: Canned chickpeas may be substituted for the dried (use 4 cups canned chickpeas). Be sure to rinse them thoroughly. Purée a small portion of the soup for added texture. Chicken stock may replace the water for added flavor.

Ingredients

8 ounces dried chickpeas *(see Notes)*

4 garlic cloves, minced

2 tablespoons olive oil

4 ounces dry wide pasta

salt and pepper to taste

grated sharp cheese for serving

Chestnut Soup

Ingredients

1 pound fresh chestnuts *(see Notes)*

8 cups water or chicken stock

4 ounces thick bacon or pancetta, finely diced

5 sprigs fennel fronds, coarsely chopped

salt and pepper to taste

1 cup warm goat's milk *(optional)*

chopped fennel sprigs for garnish

SOUPE DE CHÂTAIGNES
MINESTRA DI CASTAGNIGNA

SERVES 6 TO 8

> Napoleon's favorite! The fall harvest of chestnuts signals the coming of this much loved soup. Never picked, chestnuts are harvested by hand only after they fall naturally from the tree.

Advance Preparation: Prepare the chestnuts by roasting until tender, 10 to 15 minutes at 350 degrees F; allow them to cool and then peel.

1. Bring the water or stock to a boil in a large saucepan and stir in the chestnuts, bacon, and fennel. Add salt and pepper to taste. Lower the heat and simmer partially covered for 45 minutes.

2. Carefully purée the soup in a blender or processor, leaving bits of chestnut for texture. Return the blended soup to the saucepan.

3. Adjust seasoning with salt and pepper. If using goat's milk, stir in just before serving.

4. Top with freshly chopped fennel and serve.

Notes: Fresh chestnuts are seasonal and are difficult to find even when in season. Dried chestnuts are available year-round, and can be obtained through Internet retailers. If using dried chestnuts, rinse them thoroughly, cover with water and simmer 10 minutes. Cover the pan, remove from the heat, and allow to stand 1 hour. Drain and reserve. The chestnuts can now be roasted, but do not have to be peeled.

Napoleon was born in Ajaccio in August of 1769 to Carlo Buonaparte and his wife Marie-Letizia. He became fiercely nationalistic toward Corsica and was very disappointed when his father chose to align with the French invaders. Carlo was so enamored with French culture that he changed the spelling of their name to Bonaparte. As he moved up the French social ladder, Carlo was able to get Napoleon into the French military academy in Brienne, the beginning of a remarkable military career for one of history's most famous generals. It is said that his mother helped to get him into the academy in her own way—having an affair with Corsica's French military governor.

Napoleon Bonaparte
15 August 1769 — 5 May 1821

Swiss Chard and Fresh Cheese Soup

SOUPE AUX BLETTES ET AU BROCCIU

MINESTRA DI CEE E CASGIU FRESCHI

SERVES 4 TO 6

Chard is commonly used in soups and as a vegetable side dish. The tender greens are separated from the thick ribs, which are never wasted. The ribs are grilled or simmered and often served with a béchamel sauce.

Advance Preparation: Separate and wash the Swiss chard. Pat dry and remove the tough ribs with a paring knife (the ribs may be reserved for another use). Coarsely chop the leaves. Drain the ricotta by placing it in a sieve lined with a coffee filter and placing the sieve over a bowl. Put in the refrigerator for at least 2 hours to drain.

1. Heat the oil in a large pot over medium heat. Stir in the bacon and cook until rendered but not browned. Add the onion and sauté over low heat until clear.

2. Raise the heat and add the chard, stirring occasionally until the leaves are wilted. Toss in the chopped tomato and herbs and stir to incorporate. Cook 1 minute over medium heat.

3. Add 6 cups cold water or stock and heat to boiling. Lower the heat to a simmer and cook 20 minutes.

4. Stir in the drained ricotta and keep warm until serving. Adjust seasoning with salt and pepper.

5. If desired, stir in one beaten egg just before serving. Serve with croutons.

Notes: For more authentic flavor, use half of the ricotta (drained) beaten with a tangy soft goat's milk cheese or sheep's milk feta. The proper cheese for this dish is fresh brocciu, which can be difficult to obtain. Another excellent substitute is a mixture of equal parts *chèvre* and French sheep's milk feta, processed with a little cream to the consistency of soft cream cheese.

✳ Ingredients

4 cups Swiss chard leaves

8 ounces whole milk ricotta

2 tablespoons olive oil

1 slice thick-cut bacon, diced

1 medium onion, finely diced

2 tablespoons chopped tomato

¼ cup chopped assorted fresh herbs, such as thyme, sage, rosemary, and mint

6 cups cold water or stock

salt and pepper to taste

1 egg (*optional*)

croutons for garnish

Fennel Soup with Rice

Ingredients

1 cup dried small white beans

2 pounds fennel bulbs

¼ cup olive oil

2 garlic cloves, minced

4 sprigs fresh thyme

1 bay leaf

1 cup medium-grain rice

extra virgin olive oil for garnish

SOUPE AU FENOUI ET RIZ
MINESTRA DI FINÓCHJU E RISU

SERVES 6 TO 8

All parts of the fennel plant are used in Corsican cuisine. Fennel seeds, fronds, and bulbs are integral parts of soups, stews, and charcouterie. Along with dry pasta, rice is often added to a soup toward the end of cooking, to give the soup, which may be the main meal of the day, a heartiness.

Advance Preparation: Soak the beans in cold water for 30 minutes. Rinse and drain. Clean and thinly slice the fennel bulbs, reserving the fronds for another use.

1. Heat the oil in a large pot over medium heat. Add the sliced fennel bulbs and stir. Cook until the fennel is soft, but not browned.
2. Add the soaked beans, garlic, thyme, and bay leaf, and cook, stirring occasionally, for 2 minutes.
3. Increase the heat and add 8 cups of cold water. Stir and bring to a boil. Lower the heat and simmer 1 hour or until the beans are tender, adding the rice 15 minutes before the beans are done.
4. Add a drizzle of good quality olive oil to each bowl of soup before serving.

Notes: In a pinch, canned beans can be used, but rinse them thoroughly. Other herbs may be used in combination or alone.

Olive oil is the cooking oil of choice in Corsica and Corsican olive oil is considered among the world's best. The Olive Oil Fair, *A Festi di l'Oliu Novu*, held every March in Sainte Lucie di Tallano near Sartène, celebrates the newly pressed oil. For a historical perspective on Corsican olive oil there is an olive oil museum in the region. Corsican olive oil has recently been assigned an AOC, Appellation d' Origine Contrôlée, which signifies an official region for producing food that must meet high standards from field to package. Only when certain criteria are met can olive oil be labeled *Oliu di Corsica*.

Saint Lucie

Peasant Soup

MINESTRA D'AUTOMNE

SERVES 8

> This soup is very similar to minestrone, the classic Italian vegetable and pasta soup, reflecting Corsica's deep historical connection to Genoa prior to the eighteenth century. The ingredients are dictated by what is fresh and ready to harvest from the garden, so feel free to add some favorites of your own.

Advance Preparation: Soak the beans for 30 minutes in cold water. Drain and rinse them. Add the soaked beans to 4 cups cold water in a medium pot. Bring to a boil, lower the heat and simmer 1 hour, partially covered, adding water as necessary.

1. While the beans are cooking, heat the fat or oil in a large skillet over medium heat. Add the leeks and onion and sauté until clear but not browned, about 3 minutes. Add the garlic and stir.
2. Toss in the cabbage and sauté until wilted. Add the potatoes, zucchini, and tomatoes and mix thoroughly. Cook 1 minute.
3. Drain the cooked beans, discarding the cooking liquid. Put the sautéed vegetables and the drained beans in a soup pot. Add 8 cups water or stock. Toss in the bay leaf, thyme, and mint and simmer over low heat until the beans and potatoes are just cooked, about 20 minutes.
4. Add the pasta and additional water as necessary. Cook 15 minutes. Adjust seasoning with salt and pepper.

Notes: Fresh green beans, carrots, other squashes, and Swiss chard may all be added or substituted in this recipe. As an autumn soup, root vegetables may also be added, such as parsnips and turnips.

Ingredients

1 cup dried red beans

¼ cup pork fat, bacon fat, butter, or olive oil

2 leeks, white and light green parts only, washed thoroughly, sliced

1 medium onion, diced

3 garlic cloves, minced

2 cups green cabbage, cut into 1-inch squares

2 medium potatoes, peeled and diced

1 cup diced zucchini

4 roma tomatoes, peeled, seeded, and chopped

8 cups cold water or stock

1 bay leaf

4 sprigs fresh thyme

2 sprigs fresh mint

½ cup dry pasta (any shape)

salt and fresh ground pepper to taste

Creamy Yellow Squash Soup

Ingredients

4 ounces wide pasta such as *tagliatelle*

2 pounds yellow squash, cut into large cubes

1 medium onion, finely diced

2 garlic cloves

2 sprigs fresh thyme

4 cups whole milk or half and half (*see Notes*)

salt and pepper to taste

SOUPE VICOLAISE À LA COURGE

MINESTRA DI ZUCCA

SERVES 4 TO 6

Cream-style soups are evidence of the French influence on Corsican cuisine. The addition of fresh ewe's or goat's milk provides a tanginess as well as richness to this hearty soup.

Advance Preparation: Cook the pasta, drain, and reserve.

1. Put the squash, onion, garlic, and thyme in a wide skillet. Add just enough water to cover the bottom of the pan, but not the vegetables. Cover and steam the vegetables over high heat for 5 minutes or until tender.

2. Remove the thyme sprigs and put the vegetables and any steaming liquid in a blender or processor. Process the vegetables, adding the milk gradually, until smooth.

3. Return the soup to the stove and add the cooked pasta. Warm over low heat and adjust seasoning with salt and pepper.

Notes: Replace the whole milk with goat's milk for authentic and bold flavor. The vegetables may be steamed in a traditional steamer rather than in a skillet.

Fish Chowder

AZIMINU

SERVES 8

This recipe is best described as Corsican bouillabaisse. However, its ingredients are not as strictly defined as those of continental France. There are some guidelines to follow, but the ingredients will vary by town, season, and individual cook. This version lacks the anticipated addition of saffron, and instead uses fennel. It is served with a dollop of *rouille*, just as in Marseilles.

Advance Preparation: Prepare each ingredient according to the ingredients list.

1. To prepare the base, add the olive oil to a wide skillet. Over medium heat add the onion and sauté until clear but not browned. Add the garlic and briefly sauté.
2. Toss in the tomatoes, then the thyme, bay leaf, and fennel. Cook 5 minutes over low heat, stirring occasionally. Add the anise liqueur and stir briefly.
3. Add the fish fillets, squid, and crabmeat. Stir to combine and add 4 cups hot water. Stir gently and simmer partially covered over very low heat for 20 minutes.
4. Remove the herbs and carefully purée the contents of the skillet (in portions if necessary). Adjust seasoning with salt and pepper.
5. To top the soup, add the purée to a large stock pot over medium heat and stir in the 8 cups simmering salted water and the olive oil.
6. Add the shrimp and lobster. Simmer over low heat for 5 minutes. Add the fish and cook 5 minutes. Add the mussels and cook until just opened.
7. Serve immediately accompanied by a ramekin of rouille and slices of rustic bread, if desired.

Notes: Small crabs are used in the original recipe and are puréed whole. For a more authentic version, use cleaned whole fish with heads removed instead of fillets. Check for bones after puréeing.

✳ Ingredients

SOUP BASE:

¼ cup olive oil

1 large onion, diced

3 garlic cloves, peeled and crushed

4 roma tomatoes, quartered

1 sprig fresh thyme

1 small bay leaf

6 sprigs fresh fennel fronds

1 tablespoon anise-flavored liqueur, such as *pastis*

1 pound freshwater fish fillets, such as tilapia, cut into pieces

2 small squid, cut up

1 cup crabmeat

4 cups simmering water

salt and pepper to taste

THE TOP:

8 cups simmering salted water

¼ cup olive oil

1 pound raw shrimp, shells-on

1 8-ounce lobster tail, cut into sections, shell-on

1 pound firm fish, such as cod, cut into cubes

24 mussels, scrubbed and debearded

rouille for serving (*optional; see recipe page 12*)

sliced rustic bread for serving (*optional*)

Rouille

Ingredients

1 mild Serrano pepper, seeded, membrane removed, coarsely chopped (*optional*)

4 garlic cloves, bruised

1 egg yolk

½ cup stale bread, crust removed, moistened with stock or water, squeezed dry

1 cup olive oil

1 tablespoon coarse salt

SERVE WITH FISH CHOWDER (PAGE 11)

SERVES 8

1. With the food processor running, drop in the Serrano pepper and garlic. Add the egg yolk.
2. Open the processor and add the soaked bread. Process to a smooth consistency.
3. With the processor running, add the olive oil in a slow, steady stream.
4. Add the salt, cover, and refrigerate until needed.

Salads are not usually eaten as a separate course during a meal in Corsica. Traditional recipes rarely include lettuces, other than romaine. Greens are usually included in a soup or stew, which is often the mainstay of the meal. Some bread and cheese, possibly an egg, completes the typical Corsican meal. Marinated vegetables and seafood are popular, as accompaniments to the meal or as appetizers.

SALADS AND APPETIZERS

Chickpea and Roasted Red Pepper Salad

Romaine Salad with Fresh Cheese

Tomato Salad with Sliced Garlic

Potato and Mussel Salad

Lobster Salad

Olive and Goat Cheese Spread

Anchovy Dip

Stuffed Artichokes

Chickpea and Roasted Red Pepper Salad

Ingredients

½ cup roasted red peppers, thinly sliced (*either from a jar or freshly made; see Notes*)

2 cups canned chickpeas, rinsed thoroughly and drained

1 medium onion, finely diced

2 garlic cloves, minced

1 tablespoon red wine vinegar

1 tablespoon Dijon mustard

3 tablespoons olive oil

½ tablespoon dark, aromatic honey, preferably Corsican

¼ cup chopped fresh mint

salt and pepper to taste

SALADE DE POIS CHICHES ET POIVRON ROUGE

INSALATA DI CECIU I PIVERONE ROSSU

SERVES 6

Chickpeas were brought to Corsica by the Romans and are still quite popular. Corsican honey, perfumed by bees feeding on the blossoms of wild herbs, is used in the dressing. Corsican honey is prized throughout Europe.

Advance Preparation: Prepare each ingredient according to the directions in the ingredients list.

1. Toss the roasted bell pepper slices, chickpeas, onion, and garlic in a medium bowl.
2. Mix the vinegar with the mustard and then whisk in the oil to emulsify. Stir in the honey.
3. Toss the chickpea mixture with the chopped mint. Toss with the dressing.
4. Refrigerate 1 hour or more (overnight is best). Adjust seasonings with salt and pepper.

Notes: If using fresh red bell peppers, first char them over a flame until blackened. Seal them in a plastic bag to steam for 5 minutes or more. Peel the charred skin from the peppers, and then open them to remove the seeds and membranes. Cut into slices and toss with some olive oil and salt. Roasted peppers in jars are an excellent (and time-saving) substitute.

Romaine Salad with Fresh Cheese

ROMAINES AU BROCCIU

INSALATA INCU U BRUCCIU

SERVES 6

When served as a side dish, the romaine leaves are blanched and served warm. As a salad, crisp, chilled leaves are tossed in some olive oil and the cheese is crumbled over. Traditionally, brocciu would be used, but French sheep's milk feta is an excellent substitute.

Advance Preparation: Separate the leaves of romaine and wash thoroughly. Pat dry and remove the tough stems with a sharp paring knife. Chop the stems coarsely and reserve.

1. Toss the romaine leaves in a large bowl with enough good olive oil to completely coat them.
2. Toss the chopped romaine stems with the parsley and thyme. Add the salt and 2 tablespoons olive oil. Stir to combine. Add to the romaine leaves and toss gently.
3. Add the fresh ground pepper and crumbled feta and gently combine.
4. Serve on chilled plates with romaine leaves neatly arranged, topped with chopped egg.

Notes: Other fresh herbs may be added, such as mint and basil. Fresh lemon juice may be squeezed over the salad just before serving. Add crushed green olives as an authentic ingredient of Corsica.

Ingredients

1 head romaine lettuce

olive oil to coat the romaine leaves

¼ cup chopped flat leaf parsley

2 tablespoons fresh thyme leaves

½ teaspoon salt

2 tablespoons olive oil

fresh ground pepper

8 ounces sheep's milk feta cheese (French, if possible), crumbled

chopped hard-boiled egg for garnish

Tomato Salad with Sliced Garlic

Ingredients

6 medium very ripe tomatoes, thickly sliced

4 garlic cloves, very thinly sliced (*see Notes*)

4 leaves fresh basil, rolled-up and thinly sliced

3 tablespoons aged red wine vinegar

3 tablespoons olive oil

salt and pepper to taste

TOMATES EN SALADE AU L'AIL ÉMINCÉ

INSALATA INCU PUMMATA I AGLIU TAGLIA

SERVES 4

This simple dish is a traditional way of enjoying tomatoes in Corsica and a tasty way to use ripe tomatoes from the summer garden.

Advance Preparation: Prepare each ingredient according to the directions in the ingredients list.

1. Arrange the tomato slices neatly on salad plates.
2. Toss the garlic with the basil and top each tomato slice with some of this mixture.
3. Drizzle some vinegar over each tomato slice followed by olive oil.
4. Sprinkle each tomato slice with salt and pepper. Serve chilled.

Notes: If the garlic is too strong, the garlic cloves may be blanched in simmering water for a few minutes, allowed to cool, and then sliced.

Potato and Mussel Salad

SALADE DE MOULES

INSALATA INCU MUSCULE

SERVES 6

> Potatoes are a commonly used root vegetable in many of Corsica's dishes. Corsican mussels are related to Italian varieties, which have a paler shell than French mussels, with the more common blue-black color. With a few exceptions the waters of Corsica have relatively low levels of contaminants, an important consideration when eating fresh mollusks.

Advance Preparation: Soak the mussels in cold, salted water to purge them. Remove the beards. Cook the potatoes in salted water, allow to cool, and slice into rounds.

1. Mix the olive oil, vinegar, salt, and pepper together to make a dressing. Pour this over the potatoes, toss and allow to stand while preparing the mussels.
2. Place the mussels, thyme, and shallots in a heavy pot. Cover the bottom of the pan with water (do not cover the mussels). Cook on high, covered, until the mussels open. Allow the mussels to cool and remove them from the shells. Reserve the broth.
3. Carefully toss the mussels with the dressed potatoes and several tablespoons of the reserved broth. Add the parsley and adjust seasoning with salt and pepper. Serve chilled.

Notes: If fresh mussels are not available, frozen green-lipped mussels from New Zealand are a reasonable substitute. A mixture of fresh herbs can substitute for the parsley.

Ingredients

- 1½ pounds fresh mussels
- 6 medium new potatoes, peeled
- ¼ cup olive oil
- ¼ cup cider vinegar
- salt and pepper to taste
- 2 sprigs fresh thyme
- 3 shallots, minced
- ½ bunch flat leaf parsley, chopped

Lobster Salad

Ingredients

2 small lobsters (about 1 to 1½ pounds each)

1 celery rib, strings removed, very finely diced

1 garlic clove, finely minced

4 fresh basil leaves, rolled and thinly sliced

1 tablespoon finely chopped flat leaf parsley

1 small shallot, minced

1 teaspoon fresh lemon juice

¾ cup mayonnaise

2 tablespoons olive oil

¼ cup chopped, pitted green olives (*optional*)

salt and pepper to taste

Seafood is quite popular in Corsica and many say that the lobsters caught off its coast are the tastiest in the Mediterranean.

Advance Preparation: Steam or boil the lobsters for about 10 minutes, or until just done. Plunge the cooked lobsters into cold water. When cool, carefully remove the meat from the shell.

1. Slice the lobster tail meat into medallions. Cut the claw meat into large pieces.
2. Add the celery, garlic, basil, parsley, shallot, and lemon juice. Toss gently.
3. Beat the mayonnaise with the olive oil and add this to the lobster mixture. Toss gently to combine. Add the olives, if using, and carefully mix them in.
4. Adjust seasoning with salt and pepper. Chill thoroughly before serving.

Notes: This recipe can also make a delicious shrimp salad. Chopped walnuts make a nice textural and flavorful addition.

Olive and Goat Cheese Spread

PÂTE D'OLIVES AU FROMAGE DE CHÈVRE

PASTA D'ULIVO INCU CASGIU DI CAPRA

SERVES 4

Olives were introduced into the Corsican diet by the fifteenth century, but only since the mid-eighteenth century has olive production been a commercial venture. This recipe shows the influence of Provence, its closest regional neighbor.

Advance Preparation: Pit the olives by placing them in a resealable plastic bag and tapping on them firmly with a kitchen mallet. The pits are now easily removed with fingers.

1. Add the pitted olives to the bowl of a food processor. With the processor running, add the olive oil in a thin stream. Scrape down the bowl.
2. Add the goat cheese and thyme and pulse to form a smooth paste. Adjust seasoning with salt and pepper. Serve with crusty bread or crackers.

Notes: Fresh goat cheese (*chèvre*) is available in most markets but you should seek out locally produced artisanal cheeses at farmers' markets for an authentic addition to this recipe.

Ingredients

6 ounces pitted Niçoise or Kalamata olives (*see Advance Preparation*)

⅓ cup olive oil

6 ounces fresh goat cheese (*chèvre*), crumbled

1 teaspoon fresh thyme leaves, minced

salt and fresh ground pepper

crusty bread or crackers

Anchovy Dip

Ingredients

8 large anchovy fillets, packed in salt (*see Notes*)

1 large ripe fig

2 garlic cloves

olive oil to brush bread

slices of rustic bread

2 tablespoons finely diced onion or shallot

ANCHOÏADE
SALSA D'ANCHJOVI

SERVES 2

> There are two species of Mediterranean anchovy. The variety found along coastal waters is considered tastier and is especially enjoyed in Spain, Portugal, southern France, and Italy. A healthy anchovy population is important for predatory fish such as tuna, also popular in this region.

Advance Preparation: Carefully rinse the anchovies to remove as much salt as possible, and pat dry.

1. Put the anchovies, fig, and garlic in a food processor. Pulse to form a smooth spread.
2. Brush olive oil on the slices of bread and grill or toast the slices. Cut them into bite-size pieces.
3. Spread portions of the anchovy paste on the toast pieces and sprinkle some finely diced onion over each piece.

Notes: Try to find anchovies that are packed in salt. They will look like tiny fish, with both fillets attached, unlike those packed in oil. If using oil-packed anchovies, drain them well before using.

In Ajaccio there were only two olive groves in the early eighteenth century. One belonged to the Jesuits and the other to Napoleon Bonaparte's family. The variety grown in this region is the Zinzala olive. Today there are over 500 producers of olive oil in Corsica with more than 2,000 hectares devoted to olive trees. *A Fiera di l'Alivu* at Montemaggiore in the Balagne region is the annual olive festival, held each July.

Zinzala Olives

Stuffed Artichokes

ARTICHAUTS FARCIS
L'ARTICHJOCCI PIENI

SERVES 6

> The artichoke is primarily a Mediterranean crop, brought to Spain by the Arabs. Records show that it was cultivated in Italy by the fifteenth century, at a time when Genoa ruled Corsica. Today, in Europe, France imports the most artichokes and Spain produces the most.

Advance Preparation: Trim the bottom leaves and any large tough leaves from the artichokes. Using kitchen shears snip off any sharp points of the small leaves. Trim the stems flush with the hearts and cut the tops off, exposing the chokes. Scoop out the chokes and immediately place the artichokes into water that has been acidulated with the juice of 2 lemons to prevent browning.

1. Cook the prepared artichokes in boiling salted water for 10 minutes. Drain and reserve.
2. Mix the chopped prosciutto with the grated cheese, garlic, parsley, egg, and salt and pepper to taste. Fill each artichoke with a portion of the stuffing.
3. Heat the olive oil in a deep skillet. Sauté the pancetta for 1 minute over low heat. Add the onion and cook until clear but not browned. Stir in the tomato paste and sauté 1 minute. Add the white wine and simmer 2 minutes.
4. Place the artichokes into the sauce and add ½ cup water. Cover partially and simmer 20 minutes. Adjust seasoning with salt and pepper. Serve two stuffed artichokes with some sauce per person.

Notes: If using large artichokes, one per person should suffice. You will need to trim more large leaves, cut more sharp tips, and scoop out more choke. Increase initial boiling time by several minutes and braise for an additional 10 minutes.

Ingredients

12 baby artichokes

juice of 2 lemons

10 ounces prosciutto, finely chopped

10 ounces aged cheese, such as pecorino Romano or aged brocciu, grated

2 garlic cloves, minced

½ cup chopped flat leaf parsley

1 egg

salt and pepper

2 tablespoons olive oil

2 ounces pancetta, chopped

1 medium onion, diced

¼ cup tomato paste

1 cup dry white wine

One of the more interesting aspects of Corsican cuisine is its cooks' enthusiastic use of eggs in all manner of recipes. In addition to anticipated omelets and other breakfast-style egg dishes, Corsicans will whisk a beaten egg into a soup to enrich it or top a piece of toast with a fried egg to accompany a soup. Eggs are an excellent source of protein and the resourceful people of a harsh terrain soon realized that raising poultry— compared to livestock— required little land and feed. Desserts may also feature eggs as custard, in cheesecakes, and in tarts and turnovers.

EGGS AND OMELETS

Cured Ham Omelet
Omelet with Wild Mint
Omelet with Sea Urchins
Goat Cheese Soufflé
Sausage and Eggs
Poached Eggs on Grilled Eggplant
Eggs with Corsican Herbs

Cured Ham Omelet

FRITATTA DI PRISUTTU

SERVES 2

The hams of Corsica are known for their superior flavor, even in countries with world-class hams of their own. Corsican hams are similar to prosciutto, Bayonne, and Serrano hams, with the taste advantage of feeding the free-range pigs on chestnuts and allowing them to graze the open brush filled with wild herbs. The crisp mountain air is perfect for air drying.

Advance Preparation: Prepare each ingredient as directed in ingredients list.

1. In an omelet pan or non-stick skillet, sauté the prosciutto and onion in olive oil until the onions are clear but not browned. Add the thyme and sauté briefly.
2. Whisk the eggs with 1 tablespoon water until frothy. Add salt and pepper to taste.
3. Pour the eggs into the pan and quickly stir them into the prosciutto and onion mixture. Cook undisturbed until the eggs are set around the edge and the omelet can be turned over. Flip and continue to cook the omelet until just set.
4. Top with grated cheese, divide in half, and serve immediately.

Notes: You can use a broiler to cook the top of the omelet to avoid turning the omelet over. Consider using a mixture of herbs to top the omelet.

Ingredients

3 ounces prosciutto, chopped

2 tablespoons minced onion

2 tablespoons olive oil

1 teaspoon chopped fresh thyme leaves

4 eggs, whisked

salt and pepper

grated sharp cheese for garnish, such as Pecorino Romano

Omelet with Wild Mint

Ingredients

6 mint leaves

4 eggs, separated

¼ cup crumbled sheep's milk feta cheese (French, if available)

salt and freshly ground pepper to taste

olive oil to cook the omelet

OMELETTE AU MENTHE SAUVAGE

FRITATTA DI MENTA SALVATICU

SERVES 2

This is a classic Corsican dish. In addition to the perfume of fresh mint leaves, fresh brocciu cheese is stirred into the eggs, making hearty fare of a simple dish. Sheep's milk feta, which is more readily available that brocciu, is used in this recipe.

Advance Preparation: Pick over the mint and select superior leaves. Tear the leaves by hand into large pieces (do not use a knife). Separate eggs.

1. Beat the egg whites until soft peaks form.
2. Combine the egg yolks with the feta using a small food processor or a whisk. Gently fold the beaten egg whites into this mixture. Season with salt and pepper. Fold in the mint.
3. Heat a small amount of olive oil in an omelet pan or non-stick skillet over medium heat. Add the egg mixture and cook until the edges are set. Flip the omelet and cook until just done. Serve immediately.

Notes: For a milder flavor, substitute drained ricotta cheese for the feta or use a mixture of the two cheeses. Butter may be substituted for the olive oil to cook the omelet.

Omelet with Sea Urchins

OMELETTE AUX OURSINS

FRITATTA DI ZINU

SERVES 2

> Sea urchin roe has been popularized by the introduction of sushi to the Western palate. Known as *uni* in Japanese restaurants, many adventurous diners appreciate this exotic taste. This delicacy is not actually the eggs (roe), but the glands that produce them.

Advance Preparation: If using frozen roe, thaw in the refrigerator overnight. Gently pat each dry before using.

1. Whisk the eggs until frothy. Season with salt and pepper.
2. Heat a small amount of olive oil in a non-stick skillet or omelet pan.
3. Add the eggs and cook over medium heat just until the edges begin to set and the omelet is still very runny. Add the sea urchin roe to the omelet and continue to cook until the omelet is just set.
4. Fold the omelet in half, covering the sea urchin roe. Serve immediately.

Notes: With the increasing popularity of sushi, it may not be difficult to find sea urchin roe for this dish, well-stocked Asian markets often carry it. Some say that sea urchin roe is an acquired taste and a little goes a long way.

Ingredients

2 ounces sea urchin roe, fresh or frozen

4 eggs

salt and pepper to taste

olive oil to cook the omelet

Goat Cheese Soufflé

Ingredients

6 eggs, separated

3 tablespoons butter

3 tablespoons flour

1 cup warm milk

salt and pepper

1 tablespoon myrtle liqueur (*optional*) (*see Notes*)

4 ounces fresh goat cheese (*chèvre*), crumbled

The mountainous terrain of Corsica allows little grazing land for cows. Therefore goats and sheep form the basis for both dairy and meat dishes of the island. Ewe's and goat's milk are often mixed for brocciu, Corsica's most well-known cheese. Also produced is an excellent *chèvre* (fresh goat cheese), which is featured in this French-inspired soufflé.

Advance Preparation: Heat the oven to 325 degrees F. Butter the interior of an 8-inch soufflé dish. Separate eggs.

1. Beat the egg whites to form soft peaks. Reserve.
2. Melt the butter over low heat. Stir in the flour and cook the roux for several minutes, being careful not to brown the flour.
3. Whisk in the warm milk and cook over low heat until thickened, stirring constantly. Slowly cook the sauce for 2 minutes. Whisk in the egg yolks and cook over low heat for 1 minute (being careful not to boil). Cool to room temperature.
4. Adjust seasoning with salt and pepper. Stir in the liqueur, if using. Fold the beaten egg whites carefully into the egg mixture.
5. Sprinkle the crumbled *chèvre* into the bottom of the prepared soufflé dish. Add the egg mixture and bake at 325 degrees F for 30 minutes or until risen and set. Serve immediately.

Notes: A reasonable substitute for myrtle liqueur would be premium gin that has been heated with several leaves of rosemary (remove the rosemary and cool before using). Myrtle liqueur can be found in liquor outlets and on the Internet. The liqueur is also popular in Italy.

Sausage and Eggs

ŒUFS AU SAUCISSE SÈCHES

OVE INCU DI FIGATELLI

SERVES 2

> The sausage used for this dish in Corsica would be *figatelli*, a dried liver sausage unique to the island. It is very popular and is used in stews and soups. On Corsica, eggs are almost always cooked in olive oil; the use of butter in a dish usually indicates a recipe of French origin.

Advance Preparation: Cut the sausage into thin slices and mince the thyme.

1. Heat the oil in a skillet over medium heat. Carefully break the eggs into the pan, keeping the yolks intact.
2. Before the whites have set, place slices of sausage into the whites. Add 1 tablespoon of water to the edge of the cooking eggs and cover the pan. Cook 1 minute. The egg whites should be opaque and set.
3. Sprinkle with thyme and season with salt and pepper. Serve immediately.

Notes: A reasonable substitute for *figatelli* would be Spanish *chorizo* (not Mexican), Italian pepperoni, or any small dried salami.

Ingredients

2 ounces small dried sausage (*see Notes*)

pinch minced fresh thyme leaves

1 teaspoon olive oil

4 eggs

salt and pepper

Charcouterie is one of Corsica's most admired food products. Its hams, sausages, and other pork delicacies are renowned for exceptional flavor, imparted by the chestnuts and wild herbs that the pigs feed upon. There is a festival held in Renno, *A Tumbera*, in February. A bit gruesome to some, it celebrates the slaughtering of the pigs with a ceremony that is ostensibly outlawed by the European Union. Cooking contests and samples of all things pork, especially the famous *figatelli* sausage, abound during the festival.

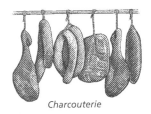

Charcouterie

Poached Eggs on Grilled Eggplant

Ingredients

1 small eggplant, peeled, cut into 4 thick slices

olive oil to coat

4 eggs

salt and pepper

olive oil for garnish

chopped herbs for garnish, such as mint, sage, and thyme

ŒUFS POCHÉS SUR AUBERGINES GRILLÉ
OVE IN CAMISGIA INCU MELZANA ABBRUSTULÌ

SERVES 2

Topping vegetables with eggs is a traditional way to increase nutritional content, turning a side dish into a substantial meal. This versatile recipe makes a tasty starter to a meal, a satisfying side dish to complete a meal of salad or soup, or a healthy start to the day.

Advance Preparation: Salt the eggplant slices thoroughly and set onto paper towels. Cover with additional paper towels and allow to stand 20 minutes. The bitter brown juices will be drawn off. Prepare the grill, if using.

1. Brush the drained eggplant slices with olive oil. Grill over coals or on a range grill, turning the slices 90 degrees to produce grill marks. Repeat on the other side. Keep warm.

2. Poach the eggs in an egg poacher or in a skillet in the vortex of simmering acidulated water.

3. Top each slice of grilled eggplant with a poached egg. Season with salt and pepper. Drizzle with olive oil, top with chopped herbs, and serve immediately.

Notes: The eggplant may be broiled or sautéed in a heavy skillet. Use additional salt carefully when finishing the dish, as the eggplant acquires salt from the draining process.

Eggs with Corsican Herbs

ŒUFS AUX HERBES CORSES
OVE INCU DI ERBIGLIE CORSA

SERVES 4

> Anyone who enjoys deviled eggs will appreciate this Corsican version. A mixture of chopped wild herbs with egg yolks provides an aromatic stuffing, and the eggs are topped with buttered breadcrumbs which are then finished in the oven.

Advance Preparation: Hard-boil the eggs (about 10 minutes) and allow to cool. Peel and reserve. Heat oven to 300 degrees F.

1. Heat 2 tablespoons of the oil in a skillet and sauté the shallots over medium heat for 1 minute. Add the Swiss chard and cook until wilted and liquid has evaporated.

2. Toss in the herbs and sauté until aromatic. Allow to cool.

3. Cut the hard-boiled eggs in half. Reserve the whites and mash the yolks with the cooled herb mixture. Add additional olive oil, if necessary. Season with salt and pepper.

4. Place the cooked egg whites on a baking dish and top each half with some of the yolk mixture. Top with breadcrumbs and drizzle each half with the remaining olive oil.

5. Bake at 300 degrees F for 10 minutes. Serve warm.

Notes: The herbs may be combined with the egg yolks in a food processor for a smoother texture. Butter may be substituted for the olive oil on top of the breadcrumbs.

Ingredients

8 eggs

4 tablespoons olive oil

2 small shallots, minced

2 cups trimmed and finely chopped Swiss chard leaves

2 sage leaves, finely chopped

1 sprig fresh thyme, leaves separated from the stems, finely chopped

2 fresh mint leaves, finely chopped

salt and pepper to taste

3 tablespoons dry unseasoned breadcrumbs

Many recipes in this section will remind you of Italian cooking, and this is where Italy's influence is greatest. But as with all Corsican recipes, there will be unexpected twists. Polenta, a staple of northern Italy, is traditionally made from cornmeal and is also popular in Corsica. Chestnut flour polenta is a unique Corsican version (although chestnut flour is expensive on the island and is used sparingly in all recipes). Toppings for polenta also vary. Game sauces are tasty additions to the porridge, as are a simple tomato sauce or some fresh brocciu.

Pasta is also loved in Corsica and again, the Italian influence is clear here. Ravioli, cannelloni, and gnocchi are all prepared in Corsica, but the fillings and toppings may be quite unexpected, such as wild boar or a sauce of kid goat. Dry pasta is almost always imported from Italy, but fresh dough is made regularly in Corsican kitchens. Wheat flour, not often used in Corsican recipes, is required for making quality fresh pasta.

Tarts and fritters are a French influence and they are enthusiastically eaten across the island. Once again, interesting differences arise among familiar recipes. A fritter batter may have wild chamomile folded in before frying. Crêpes may be cooked on a heated stone over a wood fire. Wild herbs from the *maquis* may be packed into a cheese tartlet. One of the few areas of Corsican cuisine that relies on butter is pastry and dessert recipes, reinforcing the French contribution to this cuisine.

 PASTA, FRITTERS AND TARTS

Chestnut Flour Polenta

Polenta with Grilled Corsican Ham

Potato Gnocchi with Meat Sauce

Chestnut Gnocchi with Kid Goat Ragout

Chickpea Dumplings

Gratin of Cheese and Herb Dumplings

Wild Herb Fritters

Chamomile Fritters

Cheese Crêpes Cooked on "Stone"

Cannelloni with Goat Cheese and Swiss Chard

Ravioli with Fennel and Wild Mint

Spinach and Leek Tart

Chestnut Flour Polenta

POLENTA DE FARINE DE CHÂTAIGNE

PULENDA DI FARINA CASTAGNINA

SERVES 4 TO 6

Polenta made from cornmeal is quite common to the Corsican table, but more expensive chestnut flour is used occasionally. This polenta is often served topped with fried eggs, though most popular is chestnut polenta served with (*figatelli*) sausages.

Advance Preparation: Prepare any toppings, such as fried eggs, grilled sausages, or a sauce.

1. Bring 4¼ cups salted water to a boil in a large pot. Add the chestnut flour all at once, stirring briskly.
2. Lower the heat and cook, stirring occasionally, for 20 minutes or until the polenta forms a ball and cleans the sides of the pot.
3. Turn the polenta onto a kitchen towel that has been sprinkled with chestnut flour. Cut the ball into quarters using a fine string or unflavored dental floss.
4. Cut each quarter into 1-inch-thick slices with the string, and serve alone, with butter, or with any topping desired.

Notes: Chestnut flour may be purchased over the Internet, either fine or stone-ground. Top this polenta with eggs, your favorite grilled sausages, or meat sauce. The sauces from the recipes for chestnut gnocchi (page 34) or potato gnocchi (page 33) would be excellent. Fresh goat cheese (*chèvre*) also makes a tasty topping.

✳ Ingredients

18 ounces (about 4½ cups) chestnut flour (*see Notes*)

toppings (*see Notes*)

Polenta with Grilled Corsican Ham

Ingredients

3 cups stone-ground cornmeal

6 ounces Corsican ham, Serrano ham, or prosciutto, thickly sliced

olive oil to coat serving dish

2 tablespoons butter, melted

grated Romano cheese

POLENTA AU JAMBON DE CORSE GRILLÉ
PULENDA INCU PRISUTTU DI CORSA ABRUSTULI

SERVES 4 TO 6

Cornmeal is a staple in Corsica and is often eaten as polenta. Meat sauces usually accompany cornmeal polenta, but it is often enjoyed plain, with a dab of butter and a grating of cheese. Grilled ham or sausages finish the dish.

Advance Preparation: Bring 4¼ cups salted water to a slow boil in a large pot.

1. Pour the cornmeal into the simmering water in a steady stream (*see Notes*), whisking constantly. Cook over low heat for 20 minutes or until the polenta leaves the sides of the pan when stirred.
2. Grill the ham or prosciutto slices briefly just to warm. Reserve.
3. Spread the cooked polenta on an oiled serving dish or board. Drizzle with melted butter.
4. Top the polenta with grated cheese and serve with grilled ham or prosciutto on the side.

Notes: Cornmeal tends to form lumps when poured into simmering water. To avoid this, you can use a double boiler. Stir the cornmeal into cold water in the top of a double boiler, place over a pan of simmering water and cook until thickened, about 20 minutes. Another method is to make a slurry with the cornmeal and half of the cold water. Then bring the remaining water to a simmer, stir in the slurry and cook for about 20 minutes.

Potato Gnocchi with Meat Sauce

GNOCCHIS DE POMME DE TERRE AU SAUCE VIANDE
GNOCCHI DI PATATA INCU SALSA CARNE

SERVES 6 TO 8

Potatoes are one of the few root vegetables that often make an appearance on the Corsican table. They are added to soups and stews, and in this recipe are the basis for traditional Italian fare. The meat sauce is simply referred to as "*jus.*" This dish is very popular in Bastia, and a more formal name for this recipe is "Gnocchi in the style of Bastia" (*Gnocchis à la Bastiaise / Gnocchi Manera Bastiaccia*).

Advance Preparation: Cut up the potatoes into large pieces and cook until fork tender. Drain and allow to cool.

1. In a large saucepan, brown the beef, chicken, lamb, and ham in the olive oil over medium heat.
2. Stir in the garlic and tomato paste. Cook over low heat for 2 minutes.
3. Add the red wine and raise the heat. Simmer 2 minutes.
4. Add enough water to cover and simmer for 1 hour, partially covered, adding water as necessary. Adjust seasoning with salt and pepper.
5. While the sauce is cooking, prepare the gnocchi dough. Mash the cooled potatoes and stir in enough flour to form a soft dough that is neither sticky nor too dry. Season with salt.
6. Divide the dough into 4 pieces and roll each into a long rope about ½-inch thick, using additional flour for dusting as you roll out the dough. Cut each rope into ½-inch segments. Press each segment with a floured thumb to flatten.
7. Drop the gnocchi, in batches, into a large pot of boiling salted water and cook until all gnocchi rise to the surface. Remove with a slotted spoon to a bowl.
8. Top cooked gnocchi with prepared meat sauce. Serve with grated cheese.

Notes: The gnocchi may be shaped into small shells for a more authentic form. Flour the cut segments and, using the back of a fork, roll each segment down toward the ends of the tines with your thumb.

Ingredients

MEAT SAUCE:

1 pound ground beef

8 ounces ground chicken or turkey

8 ounces ground lamb

4 ounces smoked ham, finely chopped

¼ cup olive oil

2 garlic cloves, minced

1 tablespoon tomato paste

1 cup red wine

salt and pepper

POTATO GNOCCHI:

1 pound russet potatoes, peeled

3 to 4 cups all-purpose flour

1 teaspoon salt

grated cheese for garnish

Admiral Lord Nelson of England came to the side of Pasquale Paoli to fight the French. One of the longest battles in which Lord Nelson was involved was the siege of Bastia, eventually won after thirty-seven days. It was during that siege that Nelson caught shrapnel in his eye, causing permanent loss of vision. Contrary to popular belief, Nelson did not wear an eye patch over the bad eye; rather he used a shade on his visor to block the sun from his good eye.

Nelson

Chestnut Gnocchi with Kid Goat Ragout

Ingredients

KID GOAT SAUCE:

2 tablespoons pork fat, lard, or olive oil

1 pound roasted goat meat, coarsely chopped (*see Notes*)

2 garlic cloves, minced

1 bay leaf

¼ cup chopped flat leaf parsley

1 tablespoon chopped fresh myrtle leaves (*optional*)

2 tablespoons chopped tomatoes

1 cup red wine

salt and pepper to taste

CHESTNUT GNOCCHI:

1 large russet potato, peeled

1 teaspoon salt

2 to 3 cups chestnut flour (preferably stone ground)

GNOCCHIS DE FARINE DE CHÂTAIGNE AU RAGOÛT DE CABRI

GNOCCHI DI FARINA CASTAGNINA INCU U TIANU DI CAPRETTU

SERVES 6 TO 8

The quintessential Corsican dish! In addition to chestnut flour, this dish features goat meat. With little pasture land available on Corsica, sheep and goats are more adaptable to rugged terrain, and are able to graze the scruffy *maquis*. Lamb and kid goat are most often featured in meat dishes here. This sauce is usually made from leftover roasted goat, which greatly enhances the flavor.

Advance Preparation: Cut the potato into large pieces and cook until just tender. Drain and allow to cool.

1. Heat the fat or oil over medium heat in a heavy saucepan. Add the goat meat and garlic and sauté briefly.
2. Add the bay leaf, parsley, myrtle (if using), and chopped tomatoes. Cook 2 minutes.
3. Add the red wine and simmer 1 minute. Add enough water to cover the ingredients and simmer 1 to 1½ hours over low heat, uncovered, adding water as necessary.
4. Adjust seasoning with salt and pepper and reserve the sauce (can be made 1 day ahead and reheated).
5. While the ragout is cooking, prepare the gnocchi. Pass the cooled potato through a ricer or mash with a fork. Season with salt and add enough chestnut flour to form a soft dough, neither sticky nor dry.
6. Divide the dough in half and roll each piece into a long rope about ½-inch in diameter. Cut each into pieces ½-inch long. Press each piece between the thumb and index finger (generously floured) to form flattened discs.
7. Cook the gnocchi in a large pot of boiling salted water, in batches, until the gnocchi float to the surface. Remove with a slotted spoon and drain.
8. Serve immediately, topped with the ragout.

Notes: Any leftover roast will do for this dish. Kid goat can usually be found in Latino supermarkets as *cabrito* and in Middle Eastern *halal* meat markets. This ragout is also excellent on chestnut flour polenta (page 31).

Chickpea Dumplings

QUENELLES DE POIS CHICHES

PULPETTA DI CECIU

SERVES 4

> The chickpea or garbanzo bean is the legume with the highest percentage of protein by weight, which makes it ideal to replace meat in the diet, either by necessity (the lean years) or desire (choosing vegetarianism). The flour is used in India (*besan* or *gram* flour) and chickpeas are enjoyed globally. Chickpeas are quite popular additions to Corsican stews and soups.

Advance Preparation: Prepare any sauce or topping for the dumplings, such as a ragoût of leeks and tomatoes.

1. In a large saucepan, stir the chickpea flour into the cold water. Heat to boiling and then lower the heat and simmer for 30 minutes, or until thickened.
2. Allow the porridge to cool and then form into 1-inch balls with oiled hands. (Alternately, a small scoop can be used to form the dumplings.)
3. Add the olive oil to a heavy skillet over high heat. When the oil is very hot, but not smoking, carefully add the dumplings. Cook briefly, stirring constantly, until crisp on the surface but not dark.
4. Remove to paper towels with a slotted spoon. Grind copious amounts of fresh pepper over the dumplings and serve hot.

Notes: Chickpea flour can be found in Indian markets or over the Internet. There are many ways to serve this recipe. Individual oiled saucers can be filled with the cooked porridge and drizzled with olive oil; or the whole porridge can be allowed to cool and then sliced and fried as above. A ragoût can be made with leeks and tomatoes, and the slices added to the simmering vegetables for a few minutes.

Ingredients

10 ounces (about 2½ cups) chickpea flour (*see Notes*)

4 cups salted cold water

¼ cup extra virgin olive oil

fresh ground pepper

Gratin of Cheese and Herb Dumplings

Ingredients

3 Swiss chard leaves

1 pound French sheep's milk feta cheese, mashed with a fork

2 eggs, beaten

½ cup chopped mixed fresh herbs, such as sage, mint, thyme, and rosemary

salt and freshly ground pepper

flour for dredging

oil to coat gratin dishes

4 ounces (8 tablespoons) butter, browned (*see Notes*)

4 ounces Pecorino Romano cheese, grated

QUENELLES DE FROMAGE ET HERBES AU GRATIN
STORZAPRETI DI BASTIA

SERVES 4

This is a classic preparation from Bastia, the unofficial business capital of the region, located in the northeast just below Cap Corse. Unlike gnocchi, these dumplings are large, about the size of an egg.

Advance Preparation: Trim the tough stems from the chard leaves. Blanch the leaves in boiling salted water for 2 minutes. Drain on paper towels. Finely chop the leaves when cool.

1. Stir the prepared chard into the mashed feta and then whisk in the eggs. Stir in the herbs and season with salt and pepper.
2. Form dumplings with the cheese mixture in the shape and size of an egg. Roll the dumplings in flour and drop them, a few at a time, into a large pot of boiling salted water. Cook until they float and remove them with a slotted spoon to drain on paper towels.
3. Oil individual gratin dishes and place several dumplings in each dish. Drizzle each with browned butter and top with grated Romano cheese.
4. Place the gratins under a broiler and cook until the tops are browned. Serve immediately.

Notes: To make browned butter, slowly melt the butter in a skillet. Gradually increase the heat to a simmer. Cook over low heat until the butter solids begin to brown and give off a nutty aroma, being careful not to burn the butter solids. Remove from the heat immediately.

Wild Herb Fritters

BEIGNETS DE HERBES SAUVAGE
FRITELLE INCU D' ERBIE DI MACCHIA

SERVES 4

> The herbs of the *maquis* define the island. They perfume the air and all that lives in Corsica. It is not uncommon to add copious amounts of chopped fresh herbs in myriad combination to soups, stews, omelets, and vegetables. Beignets are enjoyed across the island and these fritters are the perfect vehicle to enjoy the fragrant bounty of the land.

Advance Preparation: In a large bowl, sprinkle the yeast over the surface of the warm water and allow it to settle into the water. Stir to combine and then add the flour, a little at a time, forming a smooth batter. Cover with a damp cloth and allow to rise about 2 hours in a draft-free place.

1. When the batter has finished rising, stir in the salt and olive oil.
2. Beat the egg whites until stiff and fold them gently into the batter. Fold in the herbs.
3. Drop spoonfuls of batter into hot oil (360 to 375 degrees F) in batches. Cook until golden brown.
4. Drain on paper towels. Serve warm.

Notes: Any single herb or any combination will work well for the fritters. Goat cheese crumbled into the batter makes a tasty addition.

✳ Ingredients

- 1 teaspoon dry yeast
- 1¼ cups warm water (105 to 110 degrees F)
- 1¾ cups flour
- 1 teaspoon salt
- 2 tablespoons olive oil
- 2 egg whites
- ⅓ cup chopped fresh mixed herbs, such as thyme, mint, sage, rosemary, and basil
- oil for deep frying

Chamomile Fritters

Ingredients ✳

4 eggs
2 cups flour
¾ cup cold milk
pinch salt
⅓ cup chopped chamomile leaves
oil for frying

Many medicinal herbs are also culinary herbs, and several can be found in Corsican cuisine. Chamomile and myrtle are two examples. As a tea, chamomile is consumed around the world as a digestive aid and stomach calmative. It is also found in combination with other herbs of the *maquis* as a bouquet garni.

Advance Preparation: Heat the oil to 375 degrees F in a deep skillet. ·

1. Beat the eggs with a small amount of the flour. Whisk in a bit of milk. Add the salt and then the rest of the flour in stages, alternating with portions of milk, and finishing with the milk. More or less milk may be needed in order to form a smooth, thick batter.
2. Fold the chopped chamomile leaves into the batter.
3. Drop spoonfuls of the batter into the hot oil. Cook fritters until golden, turning occasionally as they cook.
4. Drain fritters on paper towels and serve warm.

Notes: In spite of being described as a "gentle" medicinal herb, there are many reports of allergic reactions to chamomile. Be aware when serving to guests or handling fresh leaves.

Corsica has megalithic statues called a *stantara*. They are massive upright cylindrical stones in the rough shape of humans made during the Bronze Age that are scattered in remote areas in the south, near Porto Vecchio. By 1500 BC, invaders to southern Corsica displaced these peoples and built dry stone towers (*torri*), with many of the stones coming from broken megaliths. The best preserved of these *torri* can be found just north of Porto Vecchio at Casteddu d'Araggiu. There is a curious museum in Filitosa, deep in the Taravo valley, with some remarkably preserved examples of *stantara*. Don't expect much in the way of information or well-labeled exhibits, but the megaliths themselves are worth the visit. Filitosa is considered a historic region and can be visited from Easter to October through the *Station Prèhistorique de Filitosa*.

Stantara

Cheese Crêpes Cooked on "Stone"

CRÊPES DE FROMAGE CUITES SUR LA PIERRE
MULLADES

SERVES 4

> Cooking on stone is a very old, traditional way for shepherds to prepare food while out in the fields. Slate stones heated over a wood fire and greased with animal fat became a simple and convenient way to cook while away from home. These large cheese crêpes originated in the mountain villages of Haute Corse, and are served to this day, especially when local festivals are celebrated.

Advance Preparation: Drain and crumble the feta, reserving the whey if using (*see Notes*).

1. Beat the eggs with the milk and ½ cup water. Stir in the flour. Any lumps will take care of themselves by allowing the batter to rest 30 minutes. Stir in the salt.
2. Mash the feta with a little of the batter to form a thin paste. Stir into the batter.
3. Heat a large non-stick griddle or skillet, coated with olive oil, over high heat. Using a ladle, pour an amount needed to make a large crêpe into the skillet. Rotate the pan to distribute the batter.
4. When the edges curl and the surface appears relatively dry, flip the crêpe and cook briefly. Remove from pan. Continue making crêpes until all of the batter is used. If serving warm, stack the crêpes on a plate, cover and keep in a low oven until finished.

Notes: In Rapale, where these crêpes are most loved, whey is used instead of water and milk. Replace the liquids in the recipe with the whey from the feta for a more authentic version. According to a longtime resident of Rapale, *"D'abord, ne lesinez-pas sur la fromage!"* ("Most important, don't skimp on the cheese!")

Ingredients

4 ounces sheep's milk feta cheese packed in whey

2 eggs

½ cup milk (*see Notes*)

¾ cup all-purpose flour

1 teaspoon salt

olive oil to cook the crêpes

Cannelloni with Goat Cheese and Swiss Chard

Ingredients

CANNELLONI DOUGH:

4 to 5 cups all-purpose flour

5 eggs

pinch salt

FILLING:

1 pound Swiss chard, rinsed, trimmed

2 thick slices stale bread

2 cups milk

1¼ pounds fresh goat cheese (*chèvre*)

1 egg

salt and pepper to taste

MUSHROOM SAUCE:

6 ounces cooked roast pork, cut into small cubes

5 ounces mushrooms, cultivated or wild (such as porcini or *cèpes*)

2 tablespoons olive oil

1 cup dry white wine

2 cups heavy cream

salt and pepper to taste

CANNELLONIS AU BROCCIU ET BLETTES

PIENU DI CANNILONI A U BROCCIU I CEE

SERVES 8

Along with lasagna, cannelloni is a classic Italian dish enjoyed across Corsica. As with many Corsican adaptations, fresh herbs find their way into the recipe, as does the local cheese, *brocciu*. This dish is topped with a rich mushroom-cream sauce, showing a French influence on an Italian recipe but using Corsican ingredients. This is the Corsican approach to many things—adopt what is useful, but maintain the regional identity.

Advance Preparation: The dough and the filling may be made one day ahead. Blanch the Swiss chard leaves for the filling in a pot of salted boiling water for 1 minute. Immediately remove them to a bowl of ice water. Coarsely chop the leaves. Reserve.

1. Prepare the dough: Place the flour in a large bowl and make a well in the center of the flour. Break the eggs into the well. Whisk the eggs and gradually stir some flour into them, leaving a containing circle of flour around the egg mixture. Add the salt. Continue to bring more flour into the egg mixture and, using your hands, add just enough flour to make a smooth, firm ball of dough.
2. Remove the dough from the bowl and knead briefly on a floured surface. There should be flour left over in the bowl. Wrap the dough in plastic wrap and allow to rest 30 minutes. When needed, roll the dough out to 18 x 24 inches and cut it into twenty-four 3 x 6-inch rectangles.
3. To prepare the filling soak the bread in the milk. When softened, pass the soaked bread through a food mill or processor. Combine the goat cheese with the reserved Swiss chard, the puréed bread, and the egg. Mix thoroughly. Season with salt and pepper. Reserve.
4. To prepare the sauce, sauté the roast pork and the mushrooms in the olive oil over medium heat until the mushrooms have released their liquid. Add the white wine and deglaze the pan. Continue to cook, reducing the liquid by half. Add the cream and reduce by half again. Adjust seasoning with salt and pepper.
5. Cook the cannelloni noodles al dente in a large pot of boiling salted water, about 8 minutes. Remove the noodles to a bowl of ice water to stop cooking. Pat dry.
6. Assemble the cannelloni by filling the cooked noodles with portions of filling and then rolling into cylinders, cigar-fashion. Place the cannelloni into individual baking dishes or a large casserole and top with sauce. Bake at 325 degrees For 15 minutes, or until warm. Serve immediately.

Notes: To save time, dry lasagna noodles or prepared pasta from the supermarket can substitute for making fresh pasta. A pasta machine is handy for rolling out homemade dough.

Ravioli with Fennel and Wild Mint

RAVIOLIS AU FENOUIL ET MENTHE SAUVAGE

RAVIOLI INCU DI FINOCHJU I MENTA SALVATICU

SERVES 8

Another traditional Italian dish, ravioli made in Corsica are stuffed with the native cheese, *brocciu*, and wild herbs, such as mint and *nepita*. This again illustrates the Corsican approach to its cuisine—borrow, if you must, but keep the local flavors in place.

Advance Preparation: Clean, wash, and finely chop the fennel bulbs and the mâche for the filling.

1. Prepare the dough: Place the flour in a large bowl and make a well in the center of the flour. Break the eggs into the well. Whisk the eggs, gradually stirring some flour into the eggs, leaving a containing circle of flour around the egg mixture. Add the salt. Continue to bring more flour into the egg mixture and, using your hands, add just enough flour to make a smooth, firm ball of dough.

2. Remove the dough from the bowl and knead briefly on a floured surface. There should be flour left over in the bowl. Wrap the dough in plastic wrap and allow to rest 30 minutes. When needed, roll the dough out ¼-inch thick and cut it into 2 x 3-inch rectangles.

3. Sauté the chopped fennel in the oil for 2 minutes, or until softened. Remove the fennel from the pan, add the mâche, and cook about 1 minute. Allow both to cool.

4. In a food processor, process the cooled vegetables with the goat cheese to form a smooth paste. Stir in the mint.

5. Place a small amount of filling on one half of each rectangle of dough. Fold the long side over and pinch the ends to seal (a fork works well for this). Repeat until all dough rectangles are used.

6. Drop the ravioli into a large pot of boiling salted water, a few at a time, and boil until they float to the surface and the edges are cooked through, about 5 minutes. Remove the cooked ravioli with a slotted spoon and drain.

7. Top the raviolis with tomato sauce and grated cheese. Serve immediately.

Notes: Sheets of fresh pasta are often available in larger supermarkets and upscale markets, as a time saver. Spinach can substitute for the chard, and other herbs may be added, especially sage.

Ingredients

DOUGH:

4 to 5 cups all-purpose flour

5 eggs

pinch salt

FILLING:

2 fennel bulbs, trimmed

8 ounces mâche (lamb's lettuce) or baby spinach, trimmed

2 tablespoons olive oil

12 ounces fresh goat cheese (*chèvre*), mashed with a fork

8 fresh mint leaves, cut into very fine strips

2 ounces pecorino Romano cheese, grated

3 cups prepared tomato sauce

Spinach and Leek Tart

Ingredients

PÂTÉ BRISÉE:

6 ounces unsalted butter, chilled thoroughly, cut into small pieces

3 cups flour

3 to 4 tablespoons ice water

FILLING:

1 pound spinach

2 large leeks, white and light green parts only, thoroughly washed

1 medium onion, finely diced

3 tablespoons olive oil

1 egg

salt and freshly ground pepper

1 egg yolk beaten with 1 teaspoon cream or water

TOURTE AU VERT DE PORTO-VECCHIO
TORTA INCU SPINACIU I PORRU

SERVES 6 TO 8

This tart is a favorite in southern Corsica, and is a specialty of the town of Porto Vecchio. For a truly authentic version, add several anchovy fillets in oil.

Advance Preparation: Thoroughly wash and dry the spinach and leeks. Slice the leeks into ½-inch rounds. Heat the oven to 400 degrees F.

1. In a bowl toss the butter with the flour. Cut the butter in with a pastry knife or fork until uniform and the mixture resembles coarse meal.
2. Add enough water to form a dough that is neither too moist nor too dry. Form into a ball, wrap in plastic wrap and allow to rest 30 minutes in the refrigerator.
3. Blanch the spinach in a pot of boiling salted water for 1 minute. Remove the spinach to a bowl of ice water to stop cooking. Drain and pat dry. Coarsely chop the cooked spinach.
4. In a medium skillet, sauté the leeks and onion in olive oil until clear but not browned. Mix in the spinach and allow the mixture to cool to room temperature. Beat in the whole egg and adjust seasoning with salt and pepper.
5. Divide the dough into two unequal parts, one being a bit larger than the other. Roll out the smaller piece of dough and line a 10-inch tart pan with this piece. Add the filling.
6. Roll the larger piece of dough about 2 inches larger than the tart pan. Cover the tart and crimp the edges to seal. Slice vents into the top pastry to allow steam to release during baking (*see Notes*).
7. Brush the tart with the egg yolk wash and bake at 400 degrees F for 30 minutes or until golden brown.

Notes: A chimney can be made to vent the steam. Fashion a piece of foil into a cylinder about 1½ inches tall. Make a slit into the top pastry and fit the chimney into the slit. Carefully remove the chimney after baking, when cooled. Alternately, consider weaving a lattice top of pastry for a professional look (and to avoid venting of the steam).

Although an island with over 600 miles of coastline, Corsica's cuisine reflects the bounty of its mountains and forests. Hunting has always been, and continues to be, an important way to put food on the table, and game birds are everywhere. Thrush, wood pigeons, blackbirds, woodcocks, partridges, and pigeons are all enjoyed in a variety of ways. In addition to roasting, braising, and on the rotisserie, these little birds are stuffed with *brocciu* and herbs, and made into pâté or *salmis* (a highly seasoned stew with red wine and wild mushrooms). Chicken dishes are prevalent here as well. Little pasture or grazing land is needed to raise chickens, and they supply eggs as a bonus. Most of the recipes in this chapter have been adapted to the American marketplace and taste. Chicken, game hen, quail, pheasant, and duck have been substituted in recipes calling for the wild fowl. Feel free to substitute any game birds available.

POULTRY AND GAME BIRDS

Roast Chicken with Sage

Chicken Breasts with Grapes

Stuffed Young Chicken with Smoked Pork Loin and Chestnuts

Chicken with Capers

Pheasant Marinated in Wine with Thyme and Bay Laurel

Ragoût of Game Hen with Myrtle

Game Hens with Olives

Quail with Bacon and Mushrooms

Quail with Lentils

Roast Duck with Cabbage

Roast Chicken with Sage

Ingredients

1 (3 to 4 pound) whole chicken

4 slices white bread, crusts removed

1 cup milk

6 whole garlic cloves, peeled

12 fresh sage leaves

¼ cup olive oil

salt and pepper

sage blossoms for garnish (*optional*)

SERVES 2

This is a very popular Corsican dish. Sage is an important herb in Corsican cuisine and is often paired with poultry. During the spring, when the wild sage is in bloom, cooks incorporate the flowers of the herbs of the *maquis* whenever possible. Sage blossom honey is a specialty here and sage blossoms also work well in poultry dishes.

Advance Preparation: Clean the cavity of the chicken and trim the wing tips. Pat dry. Soak the bread in the milk to absorb the liquid. Heat oven to 375 degrees F.

1. Loosely stuff the cavity of the chicken with the soaked bread, garlic cloves, and sage leaves (*see Notes*).
2. Place the stuffed bird in a roasting pan and drizzle the olive oil over, allowing the oil to run into the roasting pan. Rub the skin with the oil and sprinkle with salt and pepper.
3. Roast at 375 degrees F for 1 hour, or until the juices from the thigh run clear.
4. Serve sections of the chicken, sprinkled with sage blossoms, if using. Add some stuffing and garlic cloves to each plate.

Notes: Always stuff a bird just before roasting, to avoid harmful bacteria; stuff a bird with cooled stuffing for the same reason. Garnish the plates with fresh sage leaves if blossoms are unavailable.

Chicken Breasts with Grapes

ESCALLOPE DE POULET AVEC RAISINS

SCALUPPINA DI PULLASTRU INCU UVE

SERVES 4

The original recipe calls for woodcock, but small bone-in chicken breasts work well. Other small game birds that may be available, such as dove or quail, are excellent prepared in this manner. Local wines are produced all across Corsica, and grapes, raisins, grape leaves, and wine are certain additions to its recipes.

Advance Preparation: Slice grapes in half. Trim the pancetta slices to the size of the chicken breasts.

1. Heat the oil in a heavy skillet over medium-high heat. Brown the chicken breasts in the oil for 1 minute on each side. Arrange the chicken breasts skin-side up in the skillet.
2. Sprinkle each breast with salt and pepper. Top each with a slice of pancetta, and 2 sage leaves, and then cover each with 2 grape leaves.
3. Turn the heat to low, cover the pan, and cook 20 minutes, or until the chicken breasts are just done but remain moist.
4. Carefully remove the chicken breasts to warm plates.
5. Deglaze the pan over high heat with white wine, scraping the bottom of the pan. Toss in the halved grapes and cook until the grapes have warmed but are not cooked.
6. Pour the sauce over the chicken breasts, distributing the grapes equally, and garnish with thyme leaves.

Notes: Bacon, cured ham, or Canadian bacon can substitute for the pancetta. If using small game birds, stuff each cavity with pancetta. Top each with sage leaves and then wrap each bird in grape leaves. Continue as directed in the recipe above.

Ingredients

24 seedless red grapes

4 thick slices pancetta (about 4 ounces)

3 tablespoons olive oil

4 bone-in chicken breasts

salt and pepper

8 fresh sage leaves

8 grape leaves

1 cup good-quality dry white wine

thyme leaves for garnish

Stuffed Young Chicken with Smoked Pork Loin and Chestnuts

Ingredients

8 fresh or dried chestnuts

2 tablespoons olive oil

1 young chicken (*poussin*) (about 1½ pounds), cleaned, wing tips removed

salt and fresh ground pepper

2 slices white bread, crusts removed, cubed

2 tablespoons chopped fresh thyme

2 tablespoons chopped fresh sage leaves

½ cup finely diced smoked pork loin

2 garlic cloves, minced

2 tablespoons olive oil

½ teaspoon salt

thyme leaves for garnish

POUSSIN FARCI AU PORC FUMÉ ET AUX MARRONS
PULLASTRU FARZITU INCU LONZU I CASTAGNE

SERVES 2

This dish is especially popular in the fall, with chestnuts in season. It also features one of Corsica's most prized charcouterie. *Lonzu*, smoked pork loin, highlights the early Italian influence on Corsican cuisine, having been brought to the island from Genoa, where it is known as *lonzo*. Smoked pork loin is popular all across the Mediterranean and the Spanish make a similar product called *lomo*.

Advance Preparation: If using fresh chestnuts, cut an "X" in the base of each chestnut with a sharp knife. Roast the chestnuts at 425 degrees F for 15 minutes, or until tender and easy to peel. Allow to cool before peeling. If using dried chestnuts, rinse them thoroughly, and then cover with water. Simmer 10 minutes over low heat. Remove the pan from the heat and cover. Allow to stand 1 hour and then drain. Heat oven to 375 degrees F.

1. Rub the olive oil over the chicken. Season with salt and pepper.
2. Toss the prepared chestnuts with the cubed bread, thyme, sage, smoked pork loin, and garlic. Mix in the olive oil and salt and loosely stuff the chicken with this mixture just before roasting.
3. Roast the chicken at 375 degrees F for 40 minutes or until the juices from the thigh run clear. Remove the chicken from the oven and allow it to rest before carving. Remove the stuffing before cooling.
4. Cut the chicken in half, along the breastbone and backbone, using poultry shears, if available.
5. Serve with stuffing on the side. Drizzle pan juices over each half chicken and sprinkle with thyme leaves.

Notes: The soaking liquid from the dried chestnuts can be used in other dishes requiring a chestnut flavor. A large game hen can substitute for the young chicken.

Fish Chowder, *page 11*

Chickpea and Roasted Red Pepper Salad, *page 14*

Goat Cheese Soufflé, *page 26*

Poached Eggs on Grilled Eggplant, *page 28*

Chestnut Gnocchi
with Kid Goat Ragout,
page 34

Spinach and Leek Tart,
page 42

Stuffed Young Chicken with Smoked
Pork Loin and Chestnuts, *page 46*

Game Hens with Olives, *page 50*

Lamb Chops with
Red Beans and Leeks,
page 57

Braised Pork Loin
with Juniper,
page 62

Wild Boar Meatballs with Roasted Red Peppers, *page 67*

Braised Rabbit with Garlic and Wine, *page 70*

Grilled Tuna with Corsican Herbs, *page 77*

Stuffed Calamari,
page 84

Octopus
with Potatoes,
page 85

Mushrooms with Red Wine, *page 90*

Stuffed Zucchini, *page 93*

Gratin of Cauliflower with Cappicola, *page 95*

Sweet Cheese-Filled
Turnovers
page 103

Chestnut Beignets,
page 106

Chicken with Capers

POULE AUX CÂPRES

GALINA INCU U TAPPANE

SERVES 4

> Capers are the salted and pickled buds of the caper shrub. This biennial plant grows well on the rocky slopes and coastlines of the Mediterranean. They are graded by size and you may have seen the terms "capote" (~10mm) or "non-pareil" (~5mm) on a jar of capers. The smallest are most expensive, but there is little difference in flavor.

Advance Preparation: Using poultry shears remove the backbone of the hen. Cut the hen in half, down the breastbone. Trim the tips of the wings and cut each breast in half. Separate the thighs from the legs. You should have 8 pieces.

1. Heat the olive oil in a large heavy skillet or casserole dish. Brown the hen pieces over medium heat.
2. Add the onions and sauté until golden, about 3 minutes. Stir in the tomato paste and cook 1 minute, stirring occasionally.
3. Add the white wine, 1 cup of water, parsley, bay leaf, and thyme sprigs. Gently stir and raise the heat until the sauce comes to a boil. Reduce the heat and simmer 1 hour, covered, adding water as necessary.
4. After the hen cooks for 1 hour, stir in the capers and cook an additional 20 minutes. Adjust seasoning with salt and pepper. Rice would make a tasty accompaniment, soaking up the luscious sauce.

Notes: To reduce the acidity and saltiness of capers, rinse them under running water before using. Otherwise just drain them for maximum flavor and impact.

Ingredients

- 1 hen (about 4 pounds)
- ⅓ cup olive oil
- 1 pound whole pearl onions, peeled
- ¼ cup tomato paste
- 2 cups dry white wine
- 1 sprig flat leaf parsley
- 1 bay leaf
- 4 sprigs fresh thyme
- ⅔ cup drained capers (*see Notes*)
- salt and pepper

Pheasant Marinated in Wine with Thyme and Bay Laurel

Ingredients

2 bone-in pheasant breasts

1 cup dry red wine, preferably Italian

2 tablespoons minced onion

3 garlic cloves, peeled and crushed

4 bay leaves

4 sprigs fresh thyme

olive oil to coat pheasant breasts for grilling

salt and pepper

thyme leaves for garnish

ground bay leaf for garnish (*optional*)

FAISAN MARINÉ EN VIN AU THYM ET LAURIER

FASGIANU MARINATA NELLA VINU INCU ERBA BARONA I ALLORU

SERVES 4

In Corsica, blackbirds are enjoyed prepared in this manner. Bay laurel (bay leaf) is indigenous to the Mediterranean and has a long history in the region. Recognized as a medicinal herb by the ancient Greeks, bay laurel is a popular culinary herb in most countries. Though bay laurel is used sparingly in many of the world's cuisines, Corsicans appreciate bold herbal flavors and the aromatic wood added to a cooking fire imparts additional flavor to a dish.

Advance Preparation: Marinate the pheasant breasts in a mixture of the red wine, minced onion, garlic, bay leaves, and thyme for 1 hour. While pheasant breasts are marinating, prepare a charcoal fire.

1. Remove the pheasant breasts from the marinade and pat dry.
2. Rub the pheasant breasts with olive oil and sprinkle with salt and pepper.
3. Grill over a hot charcoal fire until medium rare, about 4 minutes per side.
4. Garnish pheasant breasts with thyme leaves and ground bay leaf, if using. Serve warm.

Notes: Most poultry and fowl would be excellent prepared in this manner, especially quail (as an appetizer). A drizzle of extra virgin olive oil just before serving would add an authentic touch.

Ragout of Game Hen with Myrtle

RAGOÛT DE POULET DE COURNAILLES AU MYRTE
TIANU DI PULLASTRU DI CORNOVAGLIU INCU MORTA

SERVES 2

True myrtle is a medicinal plant that is used as a culinary herb almost exclusively in Corsican cuisine. Its culinary use comes from Genoa, where it can still be found in the occasional recipe. The large Italian sausage called mortadella gets its name from the myrtle berries once used in the recipe. Myrtle leaves, berries, and the wood of the plant all find their way into Corsican cuisine, as does the liqueur flavored with myrtle's essential oils.

Advance Preparation: Clean, pat dry, and quarter the game hens.

1. Heat the olive oil in a deep heavy skillet. Brown the game hens over high heat. Lower the heat and add the bacon. Cook until rendered but not browned.

2. Add the onion and garlic and cook until the onions are soft, about 2 minutes. Remove from the heat and add the liqueur. Return to the heat and cook 1 minute.

3. Add the wine, chopped tomatoes, and myrtle berries. Lower the heat and cover the pan. Simmer 45 minutes, or until the hens are tender and the meat is pulling away from the leg bone, adding water as needed.

4. Remove the game hens and reduce the sauce if necessary. Adjust seasoning with salt and pepper. Serve the hens topped with sauce. Garnish with chopped parsley.

Notes: If myrtle berries are not available, use half the amount of juniper berries and a few needles of rosemary. As a substitute for the myrtle liqueur, use quality gin with a few rosemary needles infused. *Mirto*, an Italian myrtle liqueur, is readily available though.

Ingredients

2 game hens

3 tablespoons olive oil

1 slice bacon, chopped

1 medium onion, diced

5 garlic cloves, minced

¼ cup myrtle liqueur (*see Notes*)

1 cup dry white wine

2 tablespoons chopped tomatoes

1 tablespoon myrtle berries (*see Notes*)

salt and pepper

chopped parsley for garnish

Game Hens with Olives

Ingredients

2 game hens

2 tablespoons pork fat, bacon fat, or olive oil

1 strip thick-cut bacon, chopped

1 medium onion, finely diced

3 garlic cloves, peeled

2 sprigs fresh thyme

1 teaspoon fresh rosemary leaves

4 fresh sage leaves

6 ounces pitted green olives

4 ounces sliced mushrooms

2 tablespoons chopped tomatoes

1 cup dry red wine

salt and pepper to taste

POULET DE COURNAILLES AUX OLIVES
PULLASTRU DI CORNOVAGLIU INCU L'ALIVI

SERVES 2

> Olives are essential to Corsican cuisine. Olive oil is the primary cooking medium and Corsica's olives, a treasured gift of Provence, make their way into many game dishes. The small *picholine* olive of southern France is most common. Olives are enjoyed green and brined, as well as ripe and oil cured.

Advance Preparation: Clean and halve the game hens and remove backbones.

1. Heat the fat or oil in a heavy, deep skillet. Add the chopped bacon and cook over medium heat until rendered but not crisp. Add the onion and sauté until clear but not browned.
2. Add the halved game hens and brown on both sides, about 3 minutes. Toss in the garlic cloves and herbs. Stir to combine. Cook 1 minute.
3. Add the olives and mushrooms, and stir gently. Mix in the chopped tomatoes.
4. Increase the heat and add the red wine. Lower the heat, cover and simmer about 30 minutes, or until the meat pulls away from the leg bone. Adjust seasoning with salt and pepper.
5. Serve 2 halves per person, topped with sauce. If the sauce is too thin, it may be reduced before serving.

Notes: Green olives that have been cured in garlic, chiles, spices, or herbs add flavor to this dish. Other herbs may be added.

Quail with Bacon and Mushrooms

COLIN DE VIRGINIE AUX LARD ET CHAMPIGNONS

QUAGLIU INCU PANZETTA I FUNGU

SERVES 4

Wild mushrooms, gathered enthusiastically in the woods, are enjoyed in many ways in this mountainous region. They stand alone as a side dish or appetizer, and are added to Corsica's rich soups and stews. They find their way into stuffings for vegetables and pasta as well.

Advance Preparation: Clean quail and pat dry. Heat the oven to 350 degrees F.

1. Heat the bacon in a heavy ovenproof skillet over low heat to render the fat, but not to brown. Add the onion and cook until clear but not browned, about 2 minutes.
2. Add the olive oil and raise the heat. Add the quail and brown them on both sides.
3. Stir in the mushrooms. Add the thyme sprigs, bay leaves, and garlic slices. Reduce heat and cook 2 minutes to release the mushroom liquid.
4. In a small saucepan, melt the butter over low heat and whisk in the flour. Cook over low heat until just golden. Whisk in the wine and cook over low heat until thickened. Pour this sauce over the quail mixture.
5. Cover the pan and bake at 350 degrees F for 40 minutes, or until bubbling in the center.

Notes: If wild mushrooms are unavailable, cultivated button or crimini mushrooms make a reasonable substitute. Consider adding a few re-hydrated dried porcini mushrooms (and the soaking liquid) for additional flavor.

Ingredients

- 8 semi-boneless quail
- 6 ounces thick-cut bacon, cut into small cubes
- 1 medium onion, finely diced
- 2 tablespoons olive oil
- 4 ounces thickly sliced mushrooms, preferably porcini, morels, or other wild variety
- 4 sprigs fresh thyme
- 2 bay leaves
- 4 garlic cloves, sliced
- 2 tablespoons butter
- 2 tablespoons flour
- 1 cup dry red wine
- salt and pepper to taste

Quail with Lentils

Ingredients

1½ cups dried green lentils (*see Notes*)

8 quail

2 tablespoons olive oil

3 garlic cloves, peeled

1 cup tomato purée

4 fresh sage leaves

2 bay leaves

salt and pepper to taste

COLIN DE VIRGINIE AUX LENTILLES
QUAGLIU INCU LENTICHJE

SERVES 4

Dried bean and legumes are very common to Corsican dishes, especially in soups. They are an excellent source of protein and a substitute for meat in the diet. Filling to eat, they combine well with bold flavors.

Advance Preparation: Rinse the lentils and cover them with cold water in a medium pot. Heat to a boil and cook for 2 minutes. Reduce the heat and simmer until tender, about 10 to 20 minutes. Clean the quail and pat dry.

1. While the lentils are cooking, heat the olive oil in a heavy stove-top and oven-proof casserole or Dutch oven over medium heat. Add the quail and brown on both sides.
2. Toss in the garlic and pour the tomato purée over the quail to cover. Add 1 cup water, cover, and cook over low heat 15 minutes or until the quail are just done.
3. When the lentils are barely tender, drain and add them to the cooked quail mixture. Add the sage and bay leaves. Cover and continue to cook 10 minutes.
4. Adjust seasoning with salt and pepper. Serve warm with lentils on the side.

Notes: The three most commonly used lentils in Corsican cuisine are the red lentil, which is split and fast-cooking; the brown lentil, which gets mushy when overcooked; and the French green lentils, which have great texture and a peppery flavor.

Roast Duck with Cabbage

CANARD RÔTI AU CHOU

ANATRA ARROSTU INCU DI CARBUSGIU

SERVES 2

> Partridge are prepared in this manner in Corsica. Duck makes a reasonable substitute, as it is prepared this way in France. Braised cabbage is a common accompaniment to game dishes in Corsica.

Advance Preparation: Clean and pat dry the duck and cut out the backbone with poultry scissors. Halve the duck by cutting along the breastbone. Score the skin with a sharp knife, making hatch marks. Be careful not to cut into the flesh. Heat the oven to 400 degrees F.

1. Heat the olive oil in a large, heavy ovenproof skillet. Brown the duck halves, skin-sides first, over medium heat.

2. Add the garlic cloves and place the skillet in the 400 degrees F oven and roast for 15 minutes, uncovered.

3. Carefully remove the skillet from the oven and drain as much fat from the pan as possible. Add the chopped tomato, thyme, bay leaf, and dried chile.

4. Add the cabbage (do not mix it in) and pour in 1 cup water. Cover and bake 15 minutes more, or until the cabbage is tender.

5. Carefully remove the duck halves from the pan to serving plates. Remove the garlic cloves, carefully peel them, and add them to the serving plates.

6. Season the cabbage with salt and pepper. Remove the cabbage with a slotted spoon to the serving plates. Reduce the pan liquids and pour over the cabbage and duck.

Notes: Be careful to drain as much fat as possible from the duck and the pan before adding the cabbage. The red chile may be omitted, reduced, or increased to taste.

Ingredients

1 duckling (about 4 pounds)

2 tablespoons olive oil

6 garlic cloves, unpeeled

3 tablespoons chopped tomato

2 sprigs fresh thyme

1 bay leaf

1 teaspoon dried red chile

1 small green cabbage, cored, quartered, thickly sliced

salt and pepper to taste

Corsicans categorize their recipes for meat dishes a little differently than most. The main division is whether the animal is domesticated or game. The former are called "*viandes*" or "*animals d'élevage*" (breeding animals), and this category includes sheep, goats, and cows. Surprisingly, chickens, ducks, rabbits, and all other domestically bred animals fall into this category. *Gibier* (*game*), the other category, encompasses all wild and hunted animals, including blackbirds, woodcock, partridge, and other fowl. Wild boar, the most popular game eaten, and hedgehog are also included in this category. Corsicans have a fondness for pâté and recipes abound with pâtés of blackbird, partridge, and wild boar, among others.

Most meat dishes are prepared as a casserole or stew (*ragoût* or *tianu*), often with beans and other legumes. Local wines may be added to the stewing or braising liquid, and strong herbs complement most game dishes. Large cuts, such as haunch of wild boar, are slowly cooked over coals of aromatic woods, and recipes can be found for stuffing a leg of lamb or goat with herbs, cheeses, and smoked meats. Charcouterie is a separate category in Corsican cuisine, and it earns the admiration of the world's finest producers of hams and sausages, including Spain, other regions of France, and Italy. With wild herbs grazed upon by both wild and domestic animals, and mountain-cooled air to dry the prepared meats, the perfume that is Corsica is permanently infused into these food products.

 MEATS

Ragout of Lamb with Olives and Wild Thyme
Braised Lamb Shanks in Rosé Wine
Lamb Chops with Red Beans and Leeks
Ragout of Lamb with Fresh Peas
Stew of Kid Goat and Potatoes
Leg of Kid Goat Stuffed with Roast Pork Loin
Kid Goat with Bread and Vinegar
Braised Pork with Juniper
Smoked Pork Chops with Mushrooms
Grilled Pork Tenderloin with Muscat Cream Sauce
Pork Liver Pâté
Leg of Young Wild Boar with Myrtle
Wild Boar Meatballs with Roasted Red Peppers
Veal with Green Olives
Veal Meatballs with Fresh Tomato Sauce
Braised Rabbit with Garlic and Wine
Roast Rabbit with Mint and Goat Cheese
Hunters' Stew

Ragout of Lamb with Olives and Wild Thyme

RAGOÛT D'AGNEAU AUX OLIVES ET THYM SAUVAGE

TIANU DI AGNELLU INCU ALIVI I TIMU

SERVES 4 TO 6

Lamb is a favored meat in Corsica due to mountainous terrain and limited pasture land. Animals are free to graze on a variety of aromatic herbs, depending on the season. Corsican olives and olive oil, introduced by the Genoese, are superb from the region near Balagne.

Advance Preparation: Cut the lamb into 1-inch cubes, trimming some of the fat.

1. Heat the olive oil in a large skillet over medium heat. Brown the lamb cubes, stirring occasionally.
2. Add the salt pork or bacon and sauté 2 minutes. Add the onion and sauté until translucent but not browned.
3. Sprinkle the flour over the mixture and season with salt and pepper. Stir to coat. Add the red wine and simmer until the liquid has evaporated.
4. Add the garlic, bay leaves, rosemary, thyme, tomato, and enough water to cover the meat.
5. Increase heat and bring to a boil. Then lower heat, cover the pan and simmer 1 to 1½ hours, adding liquid as necessary during the cooking process.
6. Add the olives and cook uncovered for 5 minutes, or until the sauce has thickened. Serve warm.

Notes: To peel a tomato, cut an "X" across the bottom and plunge it into simmering water for 1 minute, or until the skin has loosened. Immediately drop the tomato into ice water. The peel should slide right off. Alternately, the tomato may be charred over an open flame and the skin will blacken and slide off when cooled.

Ingredients

- 1½ pounds boneless leg of lamb
- ¼ cup olive oil
- 2 tablespoons finely diced salt pork or bacon
- 1 medium onion, finely diced
- ½ tablespoon flour
- salt and pepper
- ¼ cup red wine
- 2 garlic cloves, minced
- 2 bay leaves
- 1 tablespoon chopped fresh rosemary
- 6 sprigs fresh thyme
- 1 medium tomato, peeled, seeded, and diced (*see Notes*)
- 1 cup pitted green olives

Braised Lamb Shanks in Rosé Wine

Ingredients

¼ cup olive oil

6 lamb shanks (about 3 pounds)

¼ cup diced smoked pork loin

1 large onion, finely diced

3 garlic cloves, peeled and crushed

2 sprigs fresh thyme

1 sprig fresh rosemary

1 bay leaf

2 sprigs flat leaf parsley, chopped

salt and pepper

1 cup dry rosé wine

JARRET D'AGNEAU BRAISÉ AU VIN ROSÉ
ZANCHERETTU D'AGNELLU BRUSTA INCU DI VINU ROSSU

SERVES 6

Most of the wine produced in Corsica is consumed there. The cuisine has numerous recipes that include these local wines. They are made to be enjoyed relatively young and fresh, especially the crisp rosé, which is featured in this dish.

Advance Preparation: Prepare each ingredient as directed in the ingredients list.

1. Heat the oil in a heavy casserole or Dutch oven. Brown the lamb shanks over medium-high heat. Add the pork loin and cook 1 minute.
2. Add the onion and sauté over medium heat until soft.
3. Add the garlic, thyme, rosemary, bay leaf, and parsley. Season with salt and pepper.
4. Add ½ cup of water and the rosé wine. Bring the contents to a boil and then lower the heat. Cover and simmer 1 hour, or until the shanks are tender and pulling away from the bone.
5. Adjust seasoning with salt and pepper and serve warm.

Notes: Veal shanks work well with this dish also. Substitute red wine for rosé, if preferred. Carrots make a tasty and healthy addition. Add them 30 minutes before the shanks are done.

Lamb Chops with Red Beans and Leeks

CÔTES D'AGNEAU AUX HARICOTS ROUGE ET POIREAUX

COSTA D'AGNELLU INCU FASGIOLI ROSSU I PORRU

SERVES 4

> Dried beans are a staple of the Corsican kitchen, in myriad colors and sizes. Often found in soups and used to add protein to a meal, cooked beans are served as a side dish and included in casseroles. In this recipe the lamb chops are grilled and the beans are cooked separately.

Advance Preparation: Soak the red beans for 1 hour in cold water. Prepare a charcoal grill, if using, to cook the lamb chops.

1. Heat the oil in a heavy pot over medium heat. Add the pancetta and sauté until soft, about 2 minutes. Add the leeks and garlic and cook until the leeks are soft but not browned.
2. Drain the beans and add to the pot along with the rosemary, thyme, mint, sage, and bay leaf. Add the tomatoes and stir the mixture thoroughly.
3. Add the wine and 3 cups of water and bring to a boil. Lower the heat and simmer until the beans are tender, about 1½ hours. Adjust seasoning with salt and pepper.
4. Grill the lamb chops over hot coals, or under a broiler, to medium rare.
5. Add the grilled chops to the top of the bean pot and serve family-style.

Notes: Any dried bean will do, but pinto beans would be especially good in this recipe. The cooked beans make a tasty side dish to any main course.

Ingredients

- 2 cups dried red beans
- ⅓ cup olive oil
- 2 slices pancetta or bacon, chopped
- 4 leeks, white parts only, cleaned and sliced
- 2 garlic cloves, minced
- 1 sprig fresh rosemary
- 2 sprigs fresh thyme
- 4 fresh mint leaves
- 4 fresh sage leaves
- 1 bay leaf
- 2 roma tomatoes, peeled, coarsely chopped
- 1 cup dry white wine
- salt and pepper
- 12 small lamb loin chops (about 2 pounds)

Ragout of Lamb with Fresh Peas

Ingredients

2½ pounds fresh green peas in pods (about 1½ pounds shucked)

2 pounds boneless leg of lamb

¼ cup olive oil

2 large tomatoes, peeled, coarsely chopped

2 garlic cloves, peeled and crushed

1 large sprig fresh mint

1 cup dry white wine

1 cup beef stock

salt and pepper

RAGOÛT D'AGNEAU AUX PETITS POIS

TIANU D'AGNELLU INCU PISELLI FRESCHI

SERVES 6

In season, fresh peas are a welcome change from dried beans and legumes eaten throughout the year. They are celebrated in this dish, so be prepared to spend some time shucking them from their pods.

Advance Preparation: Shuck the peas. Cut the lamb into 1-inch cubes, trimming off some of the fat.

1. Heat the olive oil in a heavy casserole or Dutch oven. Brown the lamb cubes over medium-high heat, turning frequently.

2. Stir in the tomatoes, garlic, and mint. Add the wine and beef stock and bring to a boil. Lower the heat and cover the casserole. Simmer 1 hour, adding water as necessary.

3. When the lamb is tender, add the peas, but do not stir them in. Pour 1 cup of water into the casserole and cover. Cook 5 minutes, or until the peas are just tender, but not soft.

4. To serve, gently stir in the peas and adjust seasoning with salt and pepper.

Notes: Resist the temptation to use canned peas at all cost. Frozen peas of high quality could be used, but this dish is meant for the freshest peas available. Enlist the family to help with shucking duties.

Stew of Kid Goat and Potatoes

MÉLANGE DE CABRI ET POMMES DE TERRE

CAPRETTU IN CAZZARÓLA I POMU

SERVES 8

Potatoes are a popular root vegetable, and one of a few used regularly in Corsican cuisine. Goats are well adapted to the mountainous terrain and graze on whatever is available at that time of year, often on the wild herbs of the *maquis*.

Advance Preparation: Prepare each ingredient as directed in the ingredients list.

1. Heat the olive oil in a large, heavy skillet. Brown the meat, in batches if necessary, over medium heat.
2. Add the onion and pancetta and sauté until the onion is soft and the pancetta has rendered its fat. Deglaze the pan with the white wine.
3. Add the potatoes and tomatoes. Toss in the bay leaf, thyme, and parsley. Add enough water to cover the meat and then cover the pan.
4. Simmer the stew over low heat 45 minutes, or until the meat is tender, adding water as necessary.
5. Adjust seasoning with salt and pepper and serve piping hot.

Notes: In many Hispanic markets, kid goat (*cabrito*) may be purchased already cut into pieces. Have the butcher cut the side of goat for you, if purchasing whole.

Ingredients

- 3 tablespoons olive oil
- ½ baby goat (*cabrito*) (about 6 pounds), cut into pieces, bone-in (*see Notes*)
- 1 medium onion, finely diced
- 3 ounces pancetta or bacon, chopped
- ½ cup dry white wine
- 2 pounds potatoes, peeled and cut into large pieces
- 4 large Roma tomatoes, peeled, seeded, and quartered
- 1 bay leaf
- 4 sprigs fresh thyme
- 2 tablespoons chopped flat leaf parsley
- salt and pepper

Leg of Kid Goat Stuffed with Roast Pork Loin

Ingredients

12 ounces baby spinach

1 leg of kid goat

6 ounces smoked pork loin, coarsely ground

6 ounces ground veal or beef

6 ounces pork liver or calf's liver, minced

1 egg

1 teaspoon salt

olive oil to rub roast

salt and freshly ground pepper

JAMBE DE CABRI AU FARCIE DE LONGE DE PORC SÉCHÉE

GHJAMBA DI CAPRETTU INCU PIENU DI LONZU

SERVES 8

It is difficult to say whether lamb or kid goat is more popular in Corsica, and recipes are usually offered with directions to use either. Such is the case with this recipe. Corsicans love to use a stuffing in vegetables, fish, and large cuts of meat. They are even known to stuff their famous cheese, *brocciu*.

Advance Preparation: Blanch the spinach by plunging into a large pot of salted boiling water for 1 minute. Remove with a slotted spoon to an ice water bath. Squeeze out all water from the spinach and finely chop. Bone the leg of goat by starting at the thigh bone and working your way to the knee joint; remove the thigh bone and continue down, removing the shin and leg bone (or have your butcher bone the leg). Heat the oven to 400 degrees F.

1. Mix the pork loin with the ground veal and liver. Add the chopped spinach and egg. Add the salt and stir to make a uniform mixture.

2. Open the boned goat leg and fill the interior with the stuffing. Fold the meat over the stuffing to form a roll and then tie with kitchen twine.

3. Rub olive oil over the tied, stuffed leg and place in a large roasting pan. Roast at 400 degrees F for 40 minutes, or until the stuffing inside registers 160 degrees F.

4. Allow meat to stand 10 minutes before carving into slices. Sprinkle the roast with salt and pepper before serving.

Notes: Boneless leg of lamb is readily available and can be substituted. Leg of lamb is usually larger than a shoulder or leg of goat, so be sure to increase the amount of stuffing and the cooking time if using it.

Kid Goat with Bread and Vinegar

CABRI AU PAIN VINAIGRÉ

CAPRETTU INCU DI PANE I ACETU

SERVES 4

> This is a very old Corsican recipe, surprising in its use of so much garlic. Unlike Italian cooks, Corsicans are known to use garlic sparingly in their recipes. The vinegar used should be of the highest quality.

Advance Preparation: Cut the kid goat into large pieces leaving the bones in.

1. Heat half the olive oil in a large skillet and brown the meat over medium heat. Remove the browned pieces to a warm plate.
2. Add the remaining oil to the skillet and sauté the onion until soft but not browned. Toss in the garlic and sauté over low heat 1 minute. Return the meat to the pan.
3. Add enough water to just cover the meat. Simmer over low heat, covered, for 30 minutes.
4. Sprinkle the trimmed bread with vinegar. Allow it to soak in for a few minutes. Gently squeeze out any excess vinegar.
5. Add this bread to the skillet and stir to combine. Cook an additional 5 minutes. Adjust seasoning with salt and pepper. Stir and serve hot.

Notes: Aged red wine vinegar would be most authentic in this dish but feel free to experiment with other quality vinegars, such as cider vinegar or mild Asian rice wine vinegar.

Ingredients

2 pounds kid goat

¼ cup olive oil

1 medium onion, finely diced

12 garlic cloves, peeled

8 ounces stale bread, crust removed

½ cup good quality aged red wine vinegar

salt and pepper

Braised Pork with Juniper

Ingredients

MARINADE:

1 medium red onion, diced

2 garlic cloves, peeled and crushed

1 bay leaf

4 sprigs fresh thyme

1 sprig fresh rosemary

2 fresh sage leaves

pinch cayenne

1 cup dry red wine

½ cup myrtle liqueur (*see Notes*)

½ cup red wine vinegar

¼ cup olive oil

¼ cup dried juniper berries

4 peppercorns

½ teaspoon salt

freshly ground pepper

CASSEROLE:

2 pounds boneless pork shoulder, cut into 2-ounce pieces

3 tablespoons pork fat or olive oil

2 tablespoons flour

2 tablespoons gin

2 Roma tomatoes, quartered

1 cup dry red wine

PORC BRAISÉ AU GENIÈVRE

PORCU BRUSTA INCU PALLIOLA DI GHJINEPERU

SERVES 6

> Corsican herbs are strong, flavorful, and usually quite aromatic. Like rosemary and myrtle, juniper has a pronounced evergreen-pine essence, a flavor enjoyed in Corsican cuisine. In many recipes that call for myrtle, juniper and rosemary in combination can be a reasonable substitute.

Advance Preparation: Prepare the marinade by mixing the ingredients together in a non-reactive saucepan. Warm over low heat for 5 minutes. Allow to cool to room temperature. Add the pork and marinate for 3 to 4 hours or overnight in the refrigerator.

1. Drain the meat from the marinade. Strain the marinade through a fine sieve, saving the liquid and solids separately but tossing away the juniper berries and peppercorns.
2. Heat the pork fat or oil in a heavy casserole or Dutch oven. Pat the marinated pork dry and then brown over medium heat, turning frequently.
3. Sprinkle the flour over the meat and continue to cook, stirring frequently, until the flour has browned slightly. Remove from the heat and deglaze the pan with the gin.
4. Return to the heat and add the reserved liquid and solids from the marinade to the pan. Toss in the tomatoes, lower the heat and simmer 30 minutes, covered.
5. Add ½ cup water and the wine and gently stir the contents. Continue to simmer, covered, about 1 hour, occasionally scraping the bottom of the pan. Serve warm.

Notes: Fine quality gin infused with rosemary comes in handy when myrtle liqueur is not available (add a few needles of rosemary to warm gin and allow to steep for 30 minutes).

Smoked Pork Chops with Mushrooms

CÔTE DE PORC FUMÉ AUX CHAMPIGNONS
COSTA DI PORCU AFUMICÀ INCU FUNGI

SERVES 2

> Mushrooms require moisture, shade, and decomposing vegetation to grow. All can be found throughout the mountainous regions of Corsica. *Girolles* are the most popular mushroom eaten on the island. Also called chanterelles, *girolles* have a trumpet shape and a beautiful golden color. They first appear in late spring several days after a rainfall and grow abundantly throughout the summer.

Advance Preparation: Trim and slice the chanterelles. If using dried mushrooms (*see Notes*), soak them in warm water for 30 minutes. Save the soaking liquid to use in the recipe.

1. Heat the olive oil in a heavy deep skillet. Sauté the onions over medium heat until clear. Add the minced garlic and sauté briefly.

2. Increase the heat and add the mushrooms. Sauté over high heat 1 minute. Remove from the heat and stir in the thyme, bay leaf, and myrtle or rosemary. Set aside in a bowl.

3. Pan-fry the smoked pork chops briefly in the skillet used to cook the mushrooms.

4. Top the pork chops with the mushroom mixture and add ½ cup of water around the edge of the skillet. Simmer over low heat for 10 minutes.

5. Remove the pork chops and reduce the liquid in the skillet, if necessary. Adjust seasoning with salt and pepper.

6. Serve 2 pork chops per person, topped with mushrooms and pan juices.

Notes: As a guideline, one ounce of dried mushrooms is equivalent to 8 ounces fresh. Dried chanterelles, porcini, and morels are readily available in markets and on the Internet and can be used if fresh are not available. Always save the soaking liquid when reconstituting mushrooms and add it to the dish.

❋ Ingredients

1 pound fresh chanterelle mushrooms (*see Notes*)

¼ cup olive oil

½ cup diced onions

2 garlic cloves, minced

2 sprigs fresh thyme

1 bay leaf

1 tablespoon chopped fresh myrtle leaves or rosemary

4 smoked pork chops

salt and pepper to taste

Grilled Pork Tenderloin with Muscat Cream Sauce

Ingredients

2 tablespoons olive oil

½ cup minced red onions

1 cup finely chopped mushrooms (chanterelles preferred)

½ cup Muscat (*du Cap Corse* if available)

½ cup dry white wine

1 teaspoon fresh thyme leaves

1 teaspoon dry rubbed sage

1 cup heavy cream

salt and pepper

2 pork tenderloins (about 1½ pounds), trimmed of silver skin

FILET DE PORC GRILLÉ AU SAUCE CRÉME DU MUSCAT
FILETTU DI PORCU INCU SALSA GRETULA DI MUSCAT

SERVES 4

Cap Corse is the most northern peninsula of Corsica. It looks like a finger protruding from the northern end, and is sometimes referred to as "the island in the island." *Muscat du Cap Corse* is the famous wine of the region, made from *Muscat Blanc a Petits Graines* grapes, which are allowed to dry in the sun to concentrate sugars before pressing.

Advance Preparation: Prepare each ingredient as directed in the ingredients list. Prepare a (charcoal) grill to cook the pork tenderloin.

1. Heat the olive oil in a saucepan. Add the onions and sauté over medium heat until soft but not browned. Add the chopped mushrooms and cook until the mushrooms release their liquid, about 2 minutes. Continue to cook until the liquid has evaporated.

2. Add the Muscat and white wine and simmer to remove the alcohol. Stir in the thyme leaves and sage and cook briefly to release their aromas.

3. Add the cream and cook until reduced and the sauce coats the back of a spoon. Adjust seasoning with salt and pepper. Keep warm while grilling the pork.

4. Grill the pork tenderloins over medium coals, turning frequently, until cooked medium, about 150 degrees F in the center. Allow to stand 5 minutes before slicing.

5. Carve thick medallions of tenderloin and serve topped with the cream sauce.

Notes: Muscat from other regions of the world, especially southern France, would be suitable. Be careful to avoid overly sweet styles, such as those produced in regions using the Alexandria varietal instead of Muscat Blanc.

Pork Liver Pâté

PÂTÉ DE FOIE DE PORC

PASTIZZU DI FECATU DI MAIALE

SERVES 8

This pâté is associated with the Christmas season in Corsica, but has no symbolic meaning. The slaughter of pigs occurs at the end of autumn, and the rich pork livers, fattened by the fall chestnut harvest, are certainly not to be wasted.

Advance Preparation: Cut the pork liver and pork belly or bacon into pieces. Carefully remove any vesicles in the liver. Heat the oven to 300 degrees F.

1. Pass the pork liver, pork belly, onion, and parsley through a meat grinder or pulse the ingredients in a food processor, being careful not to purée the mixture.
2. Stir in the eggs, salt, pepper, and fennel seed.
3. Spread a light film of butter inside a pâté mold or narrow baking dish such as a loaf pan. Add some flour and rotate the pan to coat the interior. Tap out any excess flour.
4. Add the liver mixture to the mold and place the bay leaf and thyme on top. Use the reserved pork belly rind or additional strips of bacon to cover the top of the pâté.
5. Cover the mold and place it in a larger baking dish. Pour hot water into the larger pan halfway up the sides of the pâté mold.
6. Place this into the 300 degrees F oven and bake 2½ hours, adding water to the outside pan as required.
7. Remove the mold from the water bath, keep covered, and allow it to cool to room temperature.
8. Refrigerate the pâté, covered, for 24 hours before un-molding and slicing.

Notes: Liver has a thin membrane film across its surface that should be removed so the blades of your meat grinder or processor do not get entangled. For a tasty variation, the entire mold may be lined with strips of bacon before filling with the pâté mixture.

Ingredients

- 1 pound pork liver, membrane removed (*see Notes*)
- 1 pound pork belly, rind removed and reserved, or fatty bacon
- 1 small onion, quartered
- ½ cup parsley leaves
- 2 eggs
- 1 teaspoon salt
- 1 teaspoon freshly ground pepper
- 1 teaspoon ground fennel seed
- butter to coat the mold
- flour to dust the mold
- 1 bay leaf
- 2 sprigs fresh thyme

Leg of Young Wild Boar with Myrtle

Ingredients

2 cups dry red wine

2 cups water or stock

2 garlic cloves, crushed

1 small onion, quartered

1 sprig fresh myrtle or rosemary

3 bay leaves

4 myrtle or juniper berries

½ teaspoon salt

freshly ground pepper

1 small leg of wild boar (about 8 pounds)

1 bunch flat leaf parsley

1 branch myrtle or rosemary

GIGOT DE MARCASSIN AU MYRTE
CUSCIOTTU DI CIGNALETTU INCU MORTA

SERVES 8 TO 12

Young wild boars are selected for the table at less than one year of age, when they weigh about 80 to 90 pounds. A full grown wild boar can weigh as much as 300 pounds. Both are prized in Corsican cuisine. Being free to graze on wild herbs all summer and then on the fallen chestnuts in autumn, makes for very flavorful meat.

Advance Preparation: Mix the first 9 ingredients together. Marinate the leg of boar in this mixture a minimum of 4 hours or overnight in the refrigerator.

1. Prepare a charcoal grill or rotisserie. Remove the boar leg from the marinade and pat dry. Reserve the marinade.
2. Bring the marinade to a boil and then allow it to cool. Allow the meat to come to room temperature before cooking.
3. Grill or rotisserie the leg of boar to an internal temperature of 160 degrees F, basting the meat often with the cooled marinade, using a brush made from the parsley and rosemary.
4. Allow roast to stand 30 minutes before carving.

Notes: Specialty meat purveyors and Internet stores often carry wild boar. You can substitute leg of lamb or kid goat for the boar in this recipe, or use a fresh ham (picnic). The use of a brush made from herbs to baste the meat is a common Corsican practice when cooking over a fire or coals.

Wild Boar Meatballs with Roasted Red Peppers

BOULETTES DE SANGLIER AUX POIVRONS ROUGE RÔTI

"BUCCIATE" INCU A SINGHJARI DI PIVERONES ROSSU AROSTU

SERVES 4

> One common method of preparing meats is as a stew or ragout.
> Meatballs lend themselves well to this style of cooking. Beef and veal
> are also prepared in this manner and are often cooked in tomato sauce.

Advance Preparation: Char the surface of the bell peppers over an open flame
or broiler. Place them in a sealed plastic bag to steam for 10 minutes. Rub the
peppers with your hands to remove most of the charred skin. Cut the peppers
open and remove the seeds and membrane. Cut the peppers into pieces that
will fit in a processor.

1. Purée the roasted peppers in a food processor or blender, adding a few
   tablespoons of water or stock at a time to aid in blending.
2. Heat 3 tablespoons of olive oil in a heavy deep skillet. Sauté the onions over
   medium heat until clear but not browned. Add the garlic and sauté briefly.
3. Toss in the sprigs of thyme, bay leaf, and parsley and cook briefly, until
   aromatic. Add the bell pepper purée and simmer 1 minute.
4. Add 2 cups stock or water and bring to a boil. Lower the heat and simmer
   5 minutes.
5. Make the meatballs: Mix the ground boar with the garlic, chopped parsley, salt,
   and thyme leaves. Stir in the egg to a uniform mixture. Form into 1-inch balls.
6. Heat ¼ cup olive oil in a skillet. Dredge the meatballs in flour and brown
   them on all sides over medium-high heat. Remove the meatballs with a
   slotted spoon and place them in the sauce.
7. Simmer the meatballs in the red pepper sauce for 20 minutes over low heat.
   Adjust seasoning with salt and pepper. Serve warm.

Notes: Any ground meat will do for this dish. A mixture of ground pork with a
small amount of lamb would be a good substitute.

✳ Ingredients

SAUCE:

2 red bell peppers

water or stock to purée the
   peppers

3 tablespoons olive oil

½ cup diced onions

2 garlic cloves, minced

2 sprigs fresh thyme

1 bay leaf

1 sprig parsley

2 cups chicken stock or water

MEATBALLS:

1½ pounds ground wild boar
   (*see Notes*)

1 garlic clove, minced

2 tablespoons chopped parsley

1 teaspoon salt

1 teaspoon chopped fresh
   thyme leaves

1 egg

¼ cup olive oil

flour to dredge the meatballs

salt and pepper

Veal with Green Olives

Ingredients

1½ pounds boneless veal sirloin or shoulder

¼ cup olive oil

salt and pepper

1 medium onion, finely diced

2 garlic cloves, minced

1 strip pancetta or bacon, finely diced

1 cup dry red wine

¼ cup chopped tomatoes

1 bay leaf

2 sprigs fresh thyme

1 fennel bulb, white part only, sliced

¼ cup chopped fennel fronds (from the fennel bulb)

3 ounces pitted, cracked green olives (*see Notes*)

salt and pepper

VEAU AUX OLIVES VERT

VITELLU INCU L'ALIVI VERDI

SERVES 4 TO 6

With little pasture land to raise cattle, veal is both the practical way to raise beef for the table and is most tender. Veal is not served often, but when it is, it is likely to be this dish, a Corsican classic.

Advance Preparation: Cut the veal into 1-inch pieces. Prepare the other ingredients as directed in the ingredients list.

1. Heat the olive oil in a heavy casserole or Dutch oven. Add the veal and brown over medium heat. Add salt and pepper. Remove the browned meat and keep warm.

2. In the same pan, sauté the onion until soft but not browned. Stir in the garlic and cook 1 minute. Add the pancetta and cook until soft.

3. Add 2 cups of water, the wine, tomatoes, bay leaf, and thyme and stir. Add the reserved meat and bring the liquid to a boil. Lower the heat and simmer 40 minutes, adding more water as necessary.

4. Add the sliced fennel bulb and the chopped fronds. Cook an additional 20 minutes.

5. Blanch the olives in a pot of simmering water for 5 minutes. Drain and stir them into the casserole. Cook an additional 5 minutes.

6. Adjust seasoning with salt and pepper and serve warm.

Notes: In some regions, black olives are used for this dish. Feel free to use either, or a mixture of the two for a more colorful dish. For a more pronounced flavor, do not blanch the olives.

Meatballs with Fresh Tomato Sauce

BOULETTES DE VIANDE À LA SAUCE TOMATE FRAIS

"BUCCIATE" INCU A CARNE DESCU SALSA PUMATA FRESCHI

SERVES 4

> Meatballs are an economical dish, easy to prepare and well adapted to the cooking style of Corsica. They are best when simmered slowly in a flavorful sauce, and this method is used to prepare vegetables and seafood as well.

Advance Preparation: Soak the bread in the milk until the milk is absorbed. Prepare the other ingredients as directed in the ingredients list.

1. Mix the ground beef with the soaked bread, prosciutto, onion, garlic, parsley, herbs, salt, and pepper. Beat in the eggs, one at a time, forming a smooth mixture.
2. Shape the meat mixture into 2-inch balls. In a heavy skillet over medium heat, brown the meatballs in ¼ cup olive oil. Remove the meatballs and keep warm.
3. To make the sauce, in the same pan, heat the 2 tablespoons of olive oil and sauté the onions until soft. Add the garlic and sauté 1 minute. Add the chopped tomatoes, 1 cup of water, bay leaf, and sugar. Simmer sauce over low heat for 10 minutes, uncovered, stirring occasionally.
4. Add the meatballs to the sauce and cook 10 minutes, adding water as necessary. Adjust seasoning with salt and pepper. Serve warm with grated pecorino cheese.

Notes: To save time, use canned whole tomatoes instead of fresh. Look for brands with minimum salt and labeled as "organic" for best results.

Ingredients

MEATBALLS:

6 ounces stale bread, crust removed, cut into cubes

½ cup milk

1 pound ground beef (*not too lean*)

3 ounces prosciutto, finely chopped

1 medium onion, finely diced

2 garlic cloves, minced

¼ cup chopped flat leaf parsley

1 tablespoon chopped nepita or ½ tablespoon chopped fresh mint plus ½ tablespoon chopped fresh thyme

1 teaspoon salt

½ teaspoon pepper

2 eggs

¼ cup olive oil

TOMATO SAUCE:

2 tablespoons olive oil

1 medium onion, diced

3 garlic cloves, minced

6 large tomatoes, peeled, seeded, chopped (*see Notes*)

1 bay leaf

pinch of sugar

salt and pepper

grated pecorino cheese for serving

Braised Rabbit with Garlic and Wine

Ingredients

1 rabbit (about 3 pounds), dressed, cut into 6 pieces (*see Notes*)

flour to dredge the rabbit

¼ cup olive oil

6 Roma tomatoes, peeled, seeded, and quartered

6 garlic cloves, sliced

4 bay leaves

1 cup fresh sage leaves

1 cup dry white wine

salt and pepper

LAPIN À L'ETOUFFÉE AU L'AIL ET VIN
CUNIGLIULU À STUFATINU INCU AGLIU I VINU

SERVES 2 TO 3

Rabbit is enjoyed throughout Europe, but has not been as appreciated in the United States. Rabbit meat is lean and not "gamey" in flavor. It adapts well to stews and casseroles and absorbs the flavor of seasonings and marinades quite well.

Advance Preparation: Prepare the rabbit as instructed in the Notes.

1. Dredge the rabbit pieces in flour and pat off any excess.
2. Heat the olive oil in a heavy casserole dish or Dutch oven. Brown the rabbit pieces over medium heat, turning frequently. When golden, remove two-thirds of the rabbit to a warm plate.
3. Top the rabbit left in the casserole with one-third of the chopped tomatoes and garlic slices. Repeat with rabbit, tomatoes, and garlic in two more layers.
4. Toss in the bay leaves and sage and then carefully pour in the wine and 1 cup of water.
5. Bring the liquid to a boil, lower the heat, cover, and simmer 40 minutes or until tender.
6. Remove the cooked rabbit to a warm plate and reduce the sauce in the casserole. Adjust seasoning with salt and pepper. Serve the rabbit warm, topped with sauce.

Notes: Rabbit can usually be found in most large supermarkets in the frozen meat section. It can be easily sectioned with poultry shears when thawed. Separate the forelegs, the back legs, and then cut the loin (saddle) in half. Discard the ribs. A cut-up chicken can substitute for rabbit in this dish.

Roast Rabbit with Mint and Goat Cheese

LAPIN RÔTI AU MENTHE ET CHÈVRE
CUNIGLIULU INCU MENTA I CAPRA

SERVES 2 TO 3

This dish represents a modern approach to Corsican cuisine, showing a continental French influence adapted to the flavors of the isle. The recipe is simple yet elegant.

Advance Preparation: Prepare the rabbit as instructed in the Notes. Heat the oven to 350 degrees F.

1. Purée the goat cheese with the mint in a small food processor. Add milk, a little at a time, to form a smooth, spreadable paste that is not too thin. Adjust seasoning with salt and pepper.
2. Spread some of the goat cheese mixture on one side of each piece of rabbit. Place them cheese-side up in a baking dish in one layer.
3. Drizzle olive oil over the rabbit and bake at 350 degrees F for 10 minutes. Form a tent with aluminum foil and place it over the baking dish and continue to bake an additional 30 minutes. Serve warm.

Notes: Rabbit can usually be found in most large supermarkets in the frozen meat section. It can be easily sectioned with poultry shears when thawed. Separate the forelegs, the back legs, and then cut the loin (saddle) in half. Discard the ribs. To avoid the mint turning brown, mix it with the cheese immediately after chopping.

Ingredients

1 rabbit, dressed, cut into 6 pieces (*see Notes*)

6 ounces fresh goat cheese (*chèvre*)

¼ cup chopped fresh mint (*see Notes*)

milk to form a smooth paste

salt and pepper

½ cup olive oil

aluminum foil to tent the dish

Hunters' Stew

Ingredients

⅓ cup pork fat, duck fat, or olive oil

1 pound "country style" pork ribs, bone-in, cut into 1-inch pieces

1 pound beef short ribs, cut into 1-inch pieces

1 pound lamb shoulder chops, cut into 1-inch pieces

1 Cornish game hen, cut into small pieces

1 large onion, diced

2 garlic cloves, peeled and crushed

2 ounces prosciutto, chopped

2 sprigs fresh rosemary or ¼ cup myrtle leaves

6 bay leaves

½ cup chopped tomatoes

2 cups dry red wine

salt and pepper to taste

DAUBE

STUFATU

SERVES 8

This dish is simply called "stew" in Corsican, and it can contain a bit of every kind of meat found on the island. In addition to whatever is hunted that day, mutton, pork, and smoked meats are usually added.

Advance Preparation: Prepare each ingredient as directed in the ingredients list.

1. Heat the fat or oil in a heavy skillet. Brown the pork and beef ribs, lamb chops, and game hen in batches over medium heat. Reserve the meats on a warm plate.

2. In the same skillet, sauté the onion until clear but not browned. Add the garlic and prosciutto and sauté 2 minutes.

3. Toss in the rosemary and bay leaves. Add the chopped tomatoes and cook 1 minute.

4. Add the reserved meat to a large casserole or Dutch oven. Top with the tomato mixture. Add the wine and enough water to cover the meat. Bring to a boil and then lower the heat.

5. Cover the casserole and simmer 1½ hours, adding water as necessary.

6. Adjust seasoning with salt and pepper. Serve warm.

Notes: Feel free to substitute any meats desired. Replace the beef with rabbit, for example, or add some quail or pheasant. Venison would make an excellent addition and would add a more pronounced game flavor to the dish.

With over 600 miles of coastline, Corsican cuisine should be a cuisine of the sea, and yet there are more game and meat dishes cooked daily in home kitchens. For many, fish for the table comes from clear mountain streams rather than from the sea. However, Corsicans enjoy some of the highest quality seafood in the Mediterranean region, and seaside villages bring in a variety of mollusks, crustaceans, and salt-water fish to be cooked each day. They prepare the catch with traditional Corsican herbs, using olive oil as the cooking medium. Fish and seafood are prepared much the same way as meat and game. They are incorporated into thick stews, grilled over aromatic coals, stuffed with the regional cheese, or dressed with a simple sauce rich in the herbs of the *maquis*. Sardines, anchovies, eels, squid, mussels, langoustines, lobsters, cod, and a variety of small fishes such as mullet are commonly consumed from the sea. Trout, fished from pristine mountain streams, are a tasty freshwater variety enjoyed throughout the island.

FISH AND SEAFOOD

Trout Cooked on Stone

Trout in Marinade

Baked Tuna with Olives and Myrtle

Grilled Tuna with Corsican Herbs

Salt Cod with Anchovies and Tomatoes

Red Snapper with Fennel

Sardines Stuffed with Cheese

Crabs with Saffron Rice

Broiled Lobster with Myrtle and Thyme

Calamari with Tomatoes

Stuffed Calamari

Octopus with Potatoes

Mussels Corsican-Style

Fried Eels with Caper Mayonnaise

Trout Cooked on Stone

Ingredients

a large, flat stone, such as slate or flagstone, cleaned, dried, and well oiled

½ cup olive oil

4 garlic cloves, peeled

¼ cup aged red wine vinegar

¼ cup parsley

pinch salt

4 boneless whole trout, rinsed and patted dry

olive oil to brush the trout and stone

TRUITE CUITES SUR LA PIERRE
TRUITA COTTA SICURU PETRATA

SERVES 4

> Corsica's crystal clear, pure mountain streams are home to a large population of a variety of brown trout known as Corsican trout. They are delicious when prepared in a simple manner. Cooking on stone is a traditional way shepherds would cook when out in the pastures for extended periods of time; no cooking pan is required to prepare a meal.

Advance Preparation: Prepare a charcoal or wood fire and prepare the cooking stone.

1. Put the olive oil and garlic in a food processor. Blend until smooth. Add the vinegar and parsley and pulse to blend (do not purée the parsley). Add the salt and reserve the parsley sauce.
2. Heat the stone over hot coals until a drop of water "dances" across the surface. Carefully brush the hot stone with olive oil.
3. Brush the trout with olive oil and place skin-side down on the hot stone. Grill 3 minutes.
4. Brush the tops of the trout with olive oil and turn to cook an additional 3 minutes.
5. Serve the trout immediately, drizzled with the parsley sauce.

Notes: A pizza baking stone or a large cast iron skillet may substitute for the flat native stone. The dish may also be prepared over a range burner or in a hot oven.

Corsican shepherds would spend months away from home to tend their flocks. This required temporary shelter and a way to cook in extremely remote and rugged regions. Shepherds would heat a large rock slab with a wood fire underneath to use as a griddle. Animal fat would grease the surface and after years of use, the stone became seasoned like an old cast-iron skillet. This cooking technique was brought back to the home and became a popular way to cook in the villages as well. Some interesting shelters of the shepherds, called *orii*, are naturally hollowed out rocks or hollow rock formations. These shelters date as far back as the 1500s and are in such remote locations that most Corsicans today have not seen one.

Orii

Trout in Marinade

TRUITES EN ESCABÈSCHE

TRUITA IN L'AGLIOTU

SERVES 4

In the nineteenth century, it was common to preserve fish in a marinade as in this recipe. Without refrigeration, it was essential to allow a bountiful daily catch to hold for several days, and *agliotu* did this, as well as added flavor. Today preservation is not usually necessary and the marinade is often used as a sauce to dress grilled or broiled fish.

Advance Preparation: Rinse, pat dry, and open the trout. If the fish do not lie flat, cut into the backbone.

1. Heat ⅓ cup of the olive oil in a heavy skillet. Sauté the opened trout over medium heat, skin-side down, for 2 minutes. Turn and cook the flesh side an additional 2 minutes. Remove the trout to a deep non-reactive pan to be marinated.

2. Pour out the oil used to cook the fish and add half of the remaining fresh oil to the skillet. Add the garlic cloves and cook over low heat until just golden, about 5 minutes.

3. Add ⅓ cup of water and the vinegar. Bring the mixture to a boil and then lower the heat and add the bay leaf, thyme, and parsley. Simmer 2 minutes. Add the cloves and peppercorns and remove the pan from the heat. Cover and allow to steep 5 minutes.

4. Pour the marinade over the trout and allow to come to room temperature. Cover and refrigerate 5 hours or overnight. Serve cold or at room temperature with crusty bread.

Notes: Other freshwater fish, such as perch or tilapia, would be excellent prepared in this manner. If using filets, reduce cooking and marinating times accordingly. The marinade may also be used as a sauce to top grilled fish.

Ingredients

4 boneless whole trout

1 cup olive oil

6 garlic cloves, peeled

1 cup aged white wine vinegar

1 bay leaf

2 sprigs fresh thyme

2 sprigs flat leaf parsley

2 cloves

12 peppercorns

½ teaspoon salt

½ teaspoon freshly ground pepper

Crusty bread for accompaniment

Baked Tuna with Olives and Myrtle

Ingredients

2 leeks, white part only

4 (8-ounce) tuna loin steaks

olive oil to coat the tuna

1 cup pitted black olives, such as Kalamata or Niçoise

1 lemon, sliced

1 small branch fresh myrtle or rosemary

olive oil for drizzling

2 fluid ounces (1/4 cup) quality gin or myrtle liqueur

salt and pepper

THON AU FOUR AUX OLIVES ET MYRTE
TONNU A FORNU INCU D'OLIVES I MORTA

SERVES 4

Mediterranean tuna are blue fin tuna that can also be found in the eastern and western Atlantic. Blue fin tuna are endangered, but in Japan, Australia, North America, and the Mediterranean they are being cultivated, and aquaculture may help preserve this species. Yellow fin and skipjack tuna are readily available in markets.

Advance Preparation: Wash and slice the leeks. Heat the oven to 350 degrees F.

1. Rub the tuna steaks with olive oil. Place them in a large baking dish. Scatter the sliced leeks and olives over the tuna.

2. Add the lemon slices and myrtle or rosemary. Drizzle olive oil over the contents of the baking dish.

3. Bake at 350 degrees F for 15 minutes, or until the tuna is cooked medium (rosy pink in the center).

4. Remove the tuna steaks to a warm plate. Deglaze the baking dish with the gin and carefully simmer off the alcohol. Adjust seasoning with salt and pepper.

5. Top each tuna steak with lemon slices and drizzle pan juices over. Serve immediately.

Notes: The tuna may be grilled over coals and the sauce prepared separately by sautéing the leeks in olive oil and then adding the lemon slices, olives, and myrtle. Deglaze with gin and adjust seasoning with salt and pepper.

Grilled Tuna with Corsican Herbs

THON RÔTI AUX HERBES DE CORSE

TONNU ARROSTU INCU D'ERBE DI CORSE

SERVES 4

> Tuna grilled over coals is one of the best ways to enjoy this firm-fleshed fish. The sauce that accompanies it is simple to prepare and perfectly reflects the essence of Corsica—fresh herbs in abundant amounts.

Advance Preparation: Soak the slice of bread in water, squeeze dry, and chop. Prepare a charcoal grill fire.

1. Put the first 9 ingredients in a blender or food processor. Pulse to form a chunky sauce, being careful not to purée the herbs and adding more olive oil as necessary. Adjust seasoning with salt and reserve until needed.
2. Brush the tuna steaks with olive oil and grill them over hot coals 2 minutes per side for rare and 3 minutes per side for medium. Do not overcook the tuna.
3. Top each tuna steak with herb sauce and serve immediately.

Notes: The tuna may be broiled or pan seared. Be careful not to overcook the tuna; it should be rare, with a ring of cooked meat surrounding a warm, red center.

✳ Ingredients

1 thick slice of stale rustic bread

1 cup fresh basil leaves

½ cup flat leaf parsley leaves

½ cup fresh mint leaves or ¾ cup nepita

¼ cup fresh thyme leaves

¼ cup fresh myrtle leaves or rosemary leaves

2 garlic cloves, minced

½ cup olive oil (or more as required)

2 tablespoons aged red wine vinegar

Salt to taste

4 (8-ounce) tuna loin steaks

olive oil to brush tuna

salt and pepper

Salt Cod with Anchovies and Tomatoes

Ingredients

1 pound reconstituted salt cod (*see Advance Preparatio*n), cut into large pieces

12 anchovy fillets

milk to soak the anchovies

¼ cup olive oil

1 pound Roma tomatoes, peeled, seeded, and coarsely chopped

1 sprig fresh thyme

1 small fresh chile, such as Serrano, seeded and minced

¾ cup dry white wine

6 walnuts, coarsely chopped

4 garlic cloves, sliced

½ bunch flat leaf parsley, chopped, with some stems included

salt and pepper

STOCKFISH (MORUE AUX ANCHOIS ET TOMATES) U PESTU (U BACCALA INCU D'ANCHJUVA E PUMATU)

SERVES 4

One needs to be careful when discussing cod, especially the dried variety. Stockfish (*stoccafisso*) is dried cod and was a mainstay of the inland Italian diet long ago, especially on meatless Fridays. *Baccala* is salted cod, also dried, and requires a bit more soaking and changing of water to reconstitute. The original recipe calls for dried cod, and it should be used if available, but salted cod can be found in most markets.

Advance Preparation: To reconstitute the salt cod, soak it in water for 24 hours, refrigerated, changing the water several times during this period. Trim the reconstituted cod and cut into large pieces. Soak the anchovy fillets in milk for 3 hours at room temperature. Drain, rinse, and chop the anchovy fillets.

1. Put half of the olive oil in a large skillet. Add the chopped tomatoes and thyme. Sauté briefly over medium heat and then add the chile. Cook 1 minute, until fragrant.
2. Add the wine and simmer over low heat uncovered, until the tomatoes are very soft and half of the liquid has evaporated.
3. Add the reconstituted cod, the soaked and chopped anchovies, the walnuts, garlic, and parsley. Simmer over low heat about 8 minutes, drizzling in the remaining olive oil as the dish cooks.
4. Toss mixture gently and adjust seasoning with salt and pepper. Serve hot.

Notes: Salt cod is readily available in most large supermarkets as well as in ethnic Italian and Spanish markets. While fresh cod may be used (skip the reconstitution step), but the texture of reconstituted salted cod is best for this dish.

Red Snapper with Fennel

VIVANEAU AU FENOUIL

DENTICE INCU FENACHJU

SERVES 2

Fennel is a common addition to Corsican recipes. All parts are used, from the anise-flavored bulb and fronds to its seeds. The bulb is usually sliced and sautéed, the fronds added as other herbs, and the seeds can be ground to add pronounced flavor.

Advance Preparation: Prepare each ingredient as directed in the ingredients list. Prepare a charcoal fire.

1. Stuff the cavity of the snapper with the fennel fronds, fennel seeds, sliced fennel bulb, garlic, parsley, onion, and butter.
2. Secure the stuffing with toothpicks or a skewer and coat the fish with olive oil. Sprinkle with salt and pepper.
3. Grill the stuffed fish over hot coals about 6 minutes per side, until the fish is just cooked and the aroma of fennel is pronounced. Remove from the grill and serve whole on a platter.

Notes: Other small whole fish such as tilapia or catfish work well for this recipe. An excellent way to cook this dish and fish fillets in general is "*en papillote*," in a sealed foil or parchment pouch.

✳ Ingredients

- 1 red snapper (about 2 pounds), rinsed and patted dry
- 2 fennel fronds
- 1 tablespoon whole fennel seeds
- 1 fennel bulb, sliced
- 2 garlic cloves, sliced
- 1 sprig flat leaf parsley
- 1 small onion, peeled and quartered
- 2 tablespoons cold butter, cut into pieces
- olive oil to coat fish
- salt and pepper

Sardines Stuffed with Cheese

Ingredients

16 fresh sardines

4 ounces French sheep's milk feta cheese, crumbled

4 ounces fresh goat cheese (*chèvre*), crumbled

½ teaspoon chopped fresh thyme leaves

1 egg

salt and pepper

olive oil to coat sardines

½ cup dry unseasoned breadcrumbs

SARDINES FARCIES AU BROCCIU
E SARDINE PIENE INCU U BRUCCIU

SERVES 4

Sardines are enjoyed all across the Mediterranean, usually fried as an appetizer. Stuffing the fresh sardines with local cheese makes for more hearty fare. This recipe comes from Bastia, on the northern side of the island on the Mediterranean Sea.

Advance Preparation: Clean the fresh sardines and remove their heads. Heat the oven to 350 degrees F.

1. Mix the cheeses with the thyme and egg to form a smooth filling. Adjust seasoning with salt and pepper.
2. Fill each sardine cavity with a portion of the filling. Use toothpicks to close the cavities, if necessary.
3. Brush olive oil on both sides of the sardines and coat each sardine with breadcrumbs.
4. Bake the stuffed sardines at 350 degrees F for about 20 minutes. Serve hot from the oven.

Notes: Use *brocciu* if it is available in place of the feta and goat cheese. Ricotta *salata* is another good substitute for, or addition to, the mixture of cheeses. It is a dry Italian cheese, much like feta, and is usually made from ewe's milk.

Crabs with Saffron Rice

CRABES AU SAFRON RIZ

GRANCI CU U ZAFFERANU RISU

SERVES 2

> This dish reflects another influence upon Corsican cuisine, that of North Africa and Moorish Spain. More than a coloring, saffron can impart a bold medicinal flavor when overused or of poor quality. Use only the highest quality threads in all dishes calling for saffron.

Advance Preparation: Rinse, trim, and clean the crabs and pat dry.

1. Heat the olive oil in a large heavy skillet. Carefully add the crabs, upside-down, allowing the legs and claws to hang down as you place them into the pan. Cook 1 minute.
2. Add the onion, bay leaf, sage, and thyme. Toss gently over medium heat. Add the tomato and saffron and cook 1 minute.
3. Stir in the rice and cook over low heat 1 minute. Add 2 cups of water and the wine. Cover and cook 20 minutes over very low heat.
4. Remove the skillet from the heat. Toss gently and adjust seasoning with salt and pepper. Serve immediately.

Notes: Other crabs, such as stone crabs or Dungeness, would be a good substitute for the easy to eat soft-shells. Adjust portions accordingly. Never use powdered saffron, as it is often contaminated with chemicals. While expensive, a few fine saffron threads go a long way toward adding color and flavor to a recipe.

Ingredients

8 soft-shell blue crabs

¼ cup olive oil

1 large onion, diced

1 bay leaf

2 fresh sage leaves

2 sprigs fresh thyme

1 medium tomato, quartered

generous pinch saffron threads

1 cup medium grain rice, such as Valencia

1 cup dry white wine

salt and pepper

Connection to Moorish Spain is evident in the Corsican national flag. It portrays a black Moor's head wearing a white headband (*A Testa di Moru*). The head of a Moor first appeared in 1281 on Aragonese weapons and in 1297 the kings of Aragon received Sardinia and Corsica from Pope Boniface VIII. The headband was represented as a blindfold in early flags. The invading Saracens would often decapitate the Moors they were battling and the blindfolded Moor's head may represent this practice. One story of the flag's origin proposes that Corsicans decapitated the head of a Moorish chief and wrapped it in white linen. Knowing that this would not last long, they drew the blindfolded head on a white background and it became the warning symbol of Corsican resistance to all invaders. Moving the blindfold off the eyes may be a symbolic gesture of freedom from foreign conquerors. Patriot Pasquale Paoli adopted this as the flag of independent Corsica in 1762.

Testa di Moru

Broiled Lobster with Myrtle and Thyme

Ingredients

4 (2-pound) lobsters (*see Advance Preparation*)

¼ cup crème fraîche or thick heavy cream (*see Notes*)

½ teaspoon fresh thyme leaves, chopped

2 tablespoons minced shallots or sweet onion

pinch cayenne

1 teaspoon coarse grain mustard

1 tablespoon myrtle liqueur

pinch ground fennel seeds

salt and pepper

LANGOUSTE GRILLÈ AU MYRTE ET THYM
ALIGASTA INCU DI MORTA I ERBA BARONA

SERVES 4

The lobster called for in this dish is the spiny lobster of the Mediterranean. It is found from the Strait of Gibraltar to the Isle of Rhodes. Also called rock lobster, they are harvested off New Zealand and South Africa as well. Maine lobsters would also work well in this dish.

Advance Preparation: If using live lobsters, cut the lobsters in half, starting at the head, through the tail. Otherwise, ask to have the lobsters cut in half when purchasing (using them soon thereafter). Scoop out the tomalley and roe, if present. Reserve these for the topping. Heat the oven to 400 degrees F.

1. Mix the crème fraîche with the thyme, shallots, cayenne, mustard, myrtle liqueur, and fennel seeds to form a smooth sauce. Stir in the tomalley and roe, if saved.

2. Place the lobster halves, shell side down, in shallow pans and sprinkle with salt and pepper. Spread some of the topping on each lobster half.

3. Bake the lobsters at 400 degrees F for 10 minutes. To brown the topping, place the pans under a broiler for a minute. Serve immediately.

Notes: To make crème fraîche, stir one tablespoon plain yogurt with active cultures into one cup cream and allow to stand at room temperature for two hours.

Calamari with Tomatoes

ENCORNETS À LA TOMATE

TOTANU INCU DI PUMATU

SERVES 4

> Mediterranean squid are particularly rich and flavorful and are enjoyed in the cuisines of this region. Small baby squid are delicious cooked whole, and the larger ones benefit from either very brief or very long cooking times.

Advance Preparation: To clean squid, start by removing the thin skin. It easily comes off by scraping with the back of a knife. Next, twist off the tentacles. Clean the squid body by scraping firmly from the pointy tail end to the head, removing the innards. Remove the clear cuttlebone (it looks like a piece of plastic) with your fingers. Cut the body into 1-inch strips. Clean the tentacle section and remove the beak, if present. Cut the tentacle section in half.

1. In a deep skillet or casserole, sauté the onion in olive oil over medium heat until clear but not browned. Add the tomatoes and cook 2 minutes, until the tomatoes release their juice and soften.
2. Stir in the garlic, thyme, bay leaf, and rosemary. Cook until aromatic, about 2 minutes.
3. Add the water or fish stock and simmer 5 minutes. Add the prepared squid and simmer over low heat for 20 minutes, partially covered, adding more water as necessary.
4. Gently stir and adjust seasoning with salt and pepper. Serve warm.

Notes: Whole baby squid, if available, would be a tasty alternative to large squid. Baby octopus is prepared in this manner in Corsica and would also be an appropriate substitute for the squid in this recipe. The cooking time would be about the same.

Ingredients

- 1½ pounds squid, cleaned (*see Advance Preparation and Notes*)
- 1 medium onion, diced
- ¼ cup olive oil
- 6 Roma tomatoes, peeled, seeded, and chopped
- 2 garlic cloves, minced
- 2 sprigs fresh thyme
- 1 bay leaf
- 1 teaspoon chopped fresh rosemary leaves
- 2 cups water or fish stock
- salt and pepper

Stuffed Calamari

Ingredients

12 squid "tubes" (bodies),
heads, innards, and cuttlebone
removed (*see Advance
Preparation and Notes*)

1 thick slice of stale rustic bread,
crusts removed

4 ounces prosciutto, finely
chopped

1 medium onion, finely diced

2 garlic cloves, minced

⅓ cup raisins or currants

⅓ cup chopped walnuts

salt and pepper

¼ cup olive oil

3 Roma tomatoes, quartered

2 sprigs fresh thyme

1 sprig nepita or several fresh
mint leaves plus ½ teaspoon
fresh thyme leaves

ENCORNETS FARCIS

TOTANI PIENI

SERVES 4

Corsicans do love to stuff foods. They stuff legs of game, vegetables, and anything that can be a container for a tasty filling. Cheese (*brocciu*) is often the first choice for a stuffing, but these calamari are stuffed with local ham, raisins, and nuts.

Advance Preparation: Prepare the squid as directed in the Advance Preparation section for Calamari with Tomatoes on page 83 but do not cut into pieces. Soak the slice of bread in some milk and then crumble.

1. Mix the prosciutto, onion, garlic, and soaked bread together to form a smooth filling.

2. Fold in the raisins and walnuts and adjust seasoning with salt and pepper. Stuff the squid tubes with portions of this filling. Use a toothpick to close the end of each stuffed squid.

3. Heat the olive oil in a large skillet or casserole. Add the squid and the tomatoes and cook over low heat 2 minutes, until the tomatoes begin to soften, turning the squid occasionally.

4. Add the herbs and 2 cups of water. Bring to a boil, and then lower heat and simmer, covered, for 1 hour, adding water as necessary.

5. Adjust seasoning with salt and pepper and serve warm. The stuffed squid may be sliced into medallions for presentation.

Notes: Many seafood departments sell squid tubes already prepared, ready to stuff or slice into rings for fried calamari. If using whole squid, reserve the tentacles, chop them and add them to the filling with the raisins and nuts.

Octopus with Potatoes

POULPE AUX POMMES DE TERRE

U POLPU INCU I POMMI

SERVES 6

The style of this dish, "with potatoes," is a very old recipe style from the northwestern part of Corsica. The Mediterranean octopus rarely grows beyond three pounds, countering the image of giant man-eaters often portrayed in the movies.

Advance Preparation: Pound the octopus tentacles with a kitchen mallet to tenderize them. Slice them into ½-inch pieces.

1. Heat the olive oil in a large skillet. Add the sliced octopus, onion, and garlic. Sauté over medium heat 2 minutes. Add the tomatoes and cook 2 minutes.
2. Add the parsley, bay leaves, and rosemary and stir to incorporate. Add 4 cups of water and simmer, covered, about 1 hour.
3. Add the potatoes and cook an additional 20 minutes, adding more water as necessary.
4. Adjust seasoning with salt and pepper and serve warm.

Notes: Small lobsters and langoustines are also prepared in this manner. Begin with the sauce and then add the potatoes. Cut the lobsters into pieces and sauté briefly to have a bright red color. Add them to the cooking potatoes about 5 minutes before the potatoes are fork tender.

Ingredients

- 1 medium octopus (about 2 pounds), tentacles only
- ⅓ cup olive oil
- 1 medium onion, diced
- 3 garlic cloves, minced
- 3 Roma tomatoes, peeled, seeded, and chopped
- 1 sprig flat leaf parsley
- 2 bay leaves
- 1 sprig fresh rosemary
- 2 pounds new potatoes, cut into 1-inch pieces
- salt and pepper

Mussels Corsican-Style

Ingredients

2 pounds mussels in shell

4 Roma tomatoes, peeled, seeded, and chopped

¼ cup ground almonds

1 garlic clove, minced

¼ cup dry white wine

¼ teaspoon freshly ground pepper

6 large fresh basil leaves with stems, sliced

⅓ cup olive oil

1 medium onion, diced

salt and pepper

MOULES À LA CORSE
MUSCULE CU E CORSE
SERVES 2

Mediterranean mussels have a distinctive flavor, reminiscent of clams and oysters. They are fairly large and are usually farm-raised for table consumption. Mediterranean mussels are grown in southern France, Spain, Greece, and Italy, and are enjoyed in all of these countries.

Advance Preparation: Purge the mussels by soaking them in an ample amount of cold salted water for 10 minutes. Remove beards. (Beards are easily removed with pliers or an abrasive pad held between your fingers for a good grip.) Heat the oven to 375 degrees F.

1. Place the mussels in a large stock pot. Add 2 cups water and cover. Steam over high heat 5 minutes. Allow to cool slightly.

2. When cool enough to handle, remove the mussels from their shells and place them in a large gratin dish, discarding any mussels that have not opened. Strain the steaming liquid and reserve.

3. Mix half of the chopped tomatoes with the almonds, garlic, white wine, and reserved steaming liquid from the mussels. Add the pepper and basil and set aside.

4. Heat the olive oil in a heavy skillet or casserole. Sauté the onion over medium heat until soft but not browned. Add the remaining chopped tomatoes and cook over low heat 5 minutes, adding a little water if necessary.

5. Add the reserved sauce and gently stir to combine. Pour this mixture over the mussels. Bake at 375 degrees F for 10 minutes or until golden and bubbling. Serve immediately.

Notes: In a pinch, frozen mussels can be found in many seafood markets. Green-lip mussels from New Zealand are often the variety found in the freezer. Although not as good as fresh, they are convenient.

Fried Eels with Caper Mayonnaise

FRITURE D'ANGUILLES AU MAYONNAISE DE CÂPRES

FRITTURA D'ANGUILLE INCU MAIUNESA DI TAPPANU

SERVES 4

Americans have not taken to this fish, possibly due to its snake-like appearance. However, they are appreciated all across the Mediterranean. Freshwater eels are often fried, as they are in Corsica. The best are to be found in the state of Biguglia in Haute Corse.

Advance Preparation: Clean the eels and remove their heads, tails, and fins. Cut into 1-inch segments. Toss the eel sections with the thyme, rosemary, and marjoram. Add the lemon juice and a few twists of freshly ground pepper. Allow this mixture to marinate for 4 hours, refrigerated.

1. Whisk the eggs with the milk. Add the flour and stir to form a smooth batter.
2. Heat the olive oil in a deep pan to 375 degrees F. Lightly coat the marinated eel segments in batter and fry until golden, about 5 minutes. Remove with a slotted spoon to paper towels. Sprinkle with salt and pepper.
3. Beat the mayonnaise with the crushed capers and their juice. Stir in the parsley. Serve on the side as a dipping sauce for the fried eel.

Notes: Calamari would be excellent prepared in this manner. Slice prepared squid tubes into 1-inch thick rings and marinate as above for 2 hours before frying. Feel free to substitute other oils for frying, such as peanut or safflower, although olive oil will impart a more authentic taste. Homemade mayonnaise would be better than prepared, should you have the time.

Ingredients

3 pounds freshwater eels

1 teaspoon chopped fresh thyme leaves

1 teaspoon chopped fresh rosemary leaves

1 teaspoon fresh marjoram

juice of 4 lemons

freshly ground pepper

2 eggs

½ cup milk

1¼ cups flour

2 cups olive oil

salt and pepper

1 cup prepared mayonnaise

2 tablespoons capers, crushed and juice reserved

1 tablespoon chopped flat-leaf parsley

Vegetables are the mainstay of the Corsican diet, and the vegetable garden is an important part of the home. Small plots of land, demarcated by low stone walls or walls made from bricks of dry donkey or sheep manure, are passed down through family ties. The home garden is simple yet elegant in its efficient use of the land. It may start with a border of artichokes and tomatoes cascading over the reeds. Thick stakes are enveloped by a variety of beans, usually red and white varieties, including fava or broadbeans. Next, a small green field of potatoes and onions is the backdrop for four or five fruit and nut trees. More mountainous land is terraced for crops, but in either case, water is always present nearby for irrigation.

Vegetables are treated in the same manner as most Corsican recipes. They are stuffed (with *brocciu* and smoked meats), grilled over coals, or slowly cooked in stews or in casserole. Wild herbs of the *maquis* are included for flavoring, and olive oil is the medium for cooking. In addition to the vegetables mentioned above, Corsican recipes include squashes, especially zucchini and eggplant, cabbage, chard, cauliflower, and mushrooms. As with most regions of the world that have forests and rain, Corsicans appreciate harvesting mushrooms and then enjoying the bounty of the hunt in the kitchen.

VEGETABLES

Grilled Cèpes

Mushrooms with Red Wine

Eggplant Confit

Eggplant with Wild Mint

Stuffed Zucchini

Cabbage with Pancetta and Tomatoes

Gratin of Cauliflower with Cappicola

Baked Onions with Cheese

Potatoes in Ragoût

Ragoût of White Beans and Leeks

Fava Beans in Casserole with Dandelions

Rice with Olives

Grilled Cèpes

CÈPES GRILLÉS
FUNGU BULETRU ARUSTITA

SERVES 4

> Cèpes, known as porcini in Italy and boletes in North America, are universally enjoyed for their earthy, meaty flavor. These mushrooms cannot be cultivated and therefore must be hunted in forests after a rain. On Corsica, where they are found are treasured secret places not to be revealed to anyone outside of the family.

Advance Preparation: Clean the mushrooms with a damp cloth or brush (never wash or soak them in water). Trim the stems and cut the mushrooms in half. Heat the oven to 400 degrees F.

1. Grill the mushroom halves, cut side down, over hot coals until the liquid is released, about 2 minutes.
2. Arrange the grilled mushroom halves, cut-side up, in a baking dish. Sprinkle with salt and pepper.
3. Top the mushrooms with the chopped prosciutto and thyme. Cover with grated cheese.
4. Drizzle olive oil generously over the mushrooms and bake at 400 degrees F for 5 minutes, or until the cheese has melted and is golden. Serve immediately.

Notes: Cèpes (porcini) can be quite expensive when purchased fresh. Thick slices of portabella mushrooms make a reasonable substitute. Consider reconstituting a few dried porcini mushrooms and chopping them along with the prosciutto, adding the soaking liquid for additional flavor.

Ingredients

2 pounds cèpes or porcini mushrooms

salt and pepper

2 ounces prosciutto, finely chopped

2 tablespoons chopped fresh thyme leaves

4 ounces aged pecorino Romano cheese, coarsely grated

olive oil to drizzle on the mushrooms

Mushrooms with Red Wine

Ingredients

2 pounds assorted wild and cultivated mushrooms

⅓ cup olive oil

2 garlic cloves, thinly sliced

1 tablespoon chopped nepita or ½ tablespoon chopped fresh mint plus ½ tablespoon chopped fresh thyme leaves

1 cup dry red wine

salt and pepper

SERVES 4

In addition to cèpes, *girolles* or chanterelles are also gathered in Corsica and chanterelles are not prohibitively expensive, as they are now being cultivated. *Oronges* (royal agarics) are also prized by harvesters of these forest treasures, as are bluets or clitocybes. This side dish goes well with grilled and roasted game.

Advance Preparation: Clean the mushrooms with a damp cloth or brush (never wash or soak them in water). Trim the stems and cut into thick slices.

1. In a large skillet, sauté the mushrooms in the olive oil over medium-high heat until they release their liquid and soften.
2. Add the sliced garlic and chopped nepita or mixed herbs and stir. Cook 1 minute or until aromatic.
3. Add the red wine and cook over medium heat until most of the liquid has evaporated, about 5 minutes.
4. Adjust seasoning with salt and pepper. Serve immediately.

Notes: Cultivated mushrooms, such as button or crimini, work well in this dish. Consider adding a few reconstituted dry wild mushrooms for flavor, adding the soaking liquid to the pan.

Eggplant Confit

AUBERGINES CONFITES

MIRIZANI CONFITU

SERVES 4 TO 6

> Preservation is necessary where there is little refrigeration, or to make a bountiful harvest last over the winter. Eggplants are found in most vegetable gardens on the island, and the variety grown is small and tender. Where ducks are preserved in their own fat (for confit), vegetables are preserved in olive oil. This recipe will require one month to properly mellow before use.

Advance Preparation: Cut the eggplants into 1-inch pieces, sprinkle with salt and allow to drain on paper towels for 2 hours.

1. In a large saucepan, heat the vinegar to boiling. Add the eggplant pieces and simmer 3 minutes. Thoroughly drain the eggplants using a strainer or sieve.

2. Place an appropriately sized jar into boiling water for 5 minutes, along with the lid being used to seal the jar. Dry the jar and lid with a clean cloth, being careful not to touch the mouth or interior with your hands.

3. Add the eggplant pieces to the jar along with the sliced garlic, nepita or mixed herbs, and bay leaf.

4. Cover the contents of the jar with olive oil and seal. Allow to marinate 1 month before using.

Notes: This confit is enjoyed in Corsica as an accompaniment to charcouterie and cold meat dishes. Small purple Asian eggplants would be excellent in this recipe, as would baby globe eggplants. Do not use Thai eggplants as they are too bitter for this dish.

Ingredients

- 2 pounds small eggplants (*see Notes*), unpeeled
- salt to sprinkle on the eggplant pieces
- 2 cups cider vinegar
- 5 garlic cloves, thinly sliced
- 1 tablespoon chopped nepita or ½ tablespoon chopped fresh mint plus ½ tablespoon chopped fresh thyme leaves
- 1 bay leaf
- olive oil

Eggplant with Wild Mint

Ingredients

4 small eggplants

salt to sprinkle on the eggplant pieces

½ cup olive oil

6 garlic cloves, thinly sliced

2 sprigs fresh mint (wild mint, if available), finely sliced

4 Roma tomatoes, peeled, seeded, and quartered

pinch sugar

salt and freshly ground pepper

AUBERGINES AU MENTHE SAUVAGE
I MIRIZANI INCU A MENTA SALVATICU

SERVES 4

Wild mint (*Mentha arvensis*) is native to Corsica and is part of the *maquis* herbs used throughout the cuisine. Do not confuse this herb with nepita (*Calamintha Nepeta*), which is related to catnip. As with many of the native herbs used in Corsican cooking, wild mint is also considered a medicinal herb.

Advance Preparation: Peel and cut the eggplants into 1-inch pieces and toss with salt to coat each piece. Allow them to stand on paper towels to drain for 30 minutes.

1. Sauté the drained eggplant pieces in half of the oil over medium-high heat in a casserole or Dutch oven. Cook until golden but not soft. Add the garlic and mint and stir. Remove from the heat.
2. Heat the remaining oil in a skillet and add the tomatoes. Stir in the sugar and cook about 3 minutes, or until the tomatoes just soften.
3. Add the tomatoes to the casserole containing the eggplant. Gently stir and cook over low heat 5 minutes. Season with salt and pepper. Serve warm.

Notes: Wild mint may be stronger than cultivated varieties; if using, adjust amount called for in this recipe.

Stuffed Zucchini

COURGETTES AU BROCCIU

E ZUCHINE PIENE INCU U BRUCCIU

SERVES 4

Squashes are very popular in Corsica and most vegetable gardens will have zucchini growing among the eggplants. Stuffed vegetables usually have the famous Corsican cheese, *brocciu*, as a base for the filling.

Advance Preparation: Cut the zucchini in half lengthwise and drop them into salted boiling water for 3 minutes, or until just tender but firm; cool. Heat the oven to 350 degrees F.

1. When zucchini are cool, carefully scoop out some of the pulp and place it in a food processor. Add the cheeses and garlic. Pulse to incorporate.
2. Put the cheese mixture in a bowl and stir in the thyme and mint. Adjust seasoning with salt and pepper.
3. Oil the bottom of a baking dish and arrange the hollowed-out zucchini halves in the dish. Fill each with a portion of cheese mixture. Sprinkle some breadcrumbs over each piece and drizzle the remaining olive oil over.
4. Bake at 350 degrees F for 30 minutes. Serve warm.

Notes: Acorn squash or butternut squash would be excellent prepared in this manner. Increase blanching time to 5 minutes and baking time to 40 minutes for these firm-fleshed squashes. For additional texture use panko crumbs (Japanese dry breadcrumbs).

Ingredients

4 large zucchini

4 ounces French sheep's milk feta cheese

4 ounces fresh goat cheese (*chèvre*)

2 garlic cloves, minced

1 teaspoon chopped fresh thyme leaves

2 fresh mint leaves, thinly sliced

salt and pepper

3 tablespoons olive oil

dry breadcrumbs to top the zucchini

Cabbage with Pancetta and Tomatoes

Ingredients

1 medium head green cabbage, outer leaves discarded, separated into individual leaves

2 tablespoons olive oil

4 ounces pancetta, coarsely chopped

1 large onion, diced

2 small carrots, peeled and cut into ½-inch thick round slices

2 Roma tomatoes, quartered

3 garlic cloves, thinly sliced

1 sprig fresh thyme

2 bay leaves

2 cloves

pinch sugar

salt and pepper

grated Gruyère cheese as garnish

CHOU AU PANCETTA ET TOMATES
CARBUSGIU INCU PANZETTA I PUMATE

SERVES 4

> Pancetta has been prepared in Europe since medieval times. It is similar to bacon in that it is salt-cured, but is not smoked. Each comes from the same part of the pig, the pork belly. Corsican *panzetta* is most flavorful and should be sought out.

Advance Preparation: Blanch the cabbage leaves in boiling water until bright green and just beginning to soften. Drain the leaves and immediately place them into a bowl of ice water.

1. Heat the olive oil in a large casserole or skillet. Add the pancetta and sauté until soft but not browned.

2. Add the onion and sauté until the onions are translucent but not browned. Add the carrots, tomatoes, garlic, thyme, and bay leaves. Stir to combine. Cook until the tomatoes begin to soften, about 2 minutes.

3. Add the cloves and sugar. Layer the blanched cabbage leaves on top and add water to come halfway up the cabbage (do not completely cover the cabbage with water).

4. Cover the pan and cook over low heat until the cabbage and carrots are fork-tender, about 8 minutes. Check from time to time so as not to overcook the vegetables.

5. Remove the cabbage leaves to a warm platter and reduce the sauce, if necessary. Adjust seasoning with salt and pepper and top the cabbage with the sauce. Sprinkle with grated gruyère and serve immediately.

Notes: Thick sliced bacon can substitute for pancetta and it will add smokiness to this dish. Salt pork is an interesting alternative—first blanch it in boiling water for a few minutes before using.

Gratin of Cauliflower with Cappicola

CHOU-FLEUR GRATINÉ AU COPPA

CAULUFIORE CRUSTULA INCU U COPPA

SERVES 4

> Coppa, or cappicola, is charcouterie made from pork shoulder which has been dry-cured whole. In Italy (and in American delicatessens), it is rolled in paprika and spices for a piquant coating. When purchasing cappicola for Corsican dishes, buy a thick piece, un-sliced; the spicy coating can then be trimmed off.

Advance Preparation: Rinse the cauliflower and separate into florets. Remove and discard the spicy coating from the cappicola and then coarsely chop.

1. Place the cauliflower florets in boiling water and add the whole garlic clove. Simmer 3 minutes, or until the floret stems are just beginning to soften. Drain, remove the garlic clove, and place cauliflower in a gratin dish.

2. In a skillet heat the olive oil and add the chopped cappicola. Sauté over low heat for 2 minutes. Add the sliced garlic and cook until aromatic, about 1 minute.

3. Stir in the tomatoes and parsley. Add 1 cup of water and simmer 10 minutes, uncovered, adding more water as needed. Adjust seasoning with salt and pepper.

4. Top the cauliflower with the sauce and sprinkle grated cheese over the top. Broil until the cheese has melted and is bubbling. Serve immediately.

Notes: Broccoli would be tasty prepared in this manner. If cappicola is not available, prosciutto would work well.

✳ Ingredients

1 medium cauliflower, rinsed and separated into florets

2-ounce piece cappicola

1 garlic clove, peeled and left whole, plus 3 garlic cloves, peeled and thinly sliced

2 tablespoons olive oil

¼ cup chopped tomatoes

½ cup chopped flat leaf parsley

salt and pepper

grated Gruyère cheese as garnish

Baked Onions with Cheese

Ingredients

2 large onions, peeled

2 sprigs flat leaf parsley, chopped

1 ounce prosciutto, chopped

4 ounces French sheep's milk feta cheese, crumbled

1 egg, beaten

salt and pepper

olive oil

OIGNONS FARCIS AU BROCCIU

E CIVOLE PIENE INCU U BRUCCIU

SERVES 4

This recipe is a specialty of Cervione in Haute Corse. In 1975, Corsica was divided into the departments of Haute Corse and Corse-du-Sud along the historical line of demarcation by the French parliament. Before 1975, Corsica was considered both a region and a department and, at one time, was considered just a region.

Advance Preparation: Drop the onions into salted boiling water and cook for several minutes, until the onions just begin to soften but are still firm. Heat the oven to 350 degrees F.

1. Cut the onions in half, through the stem and foliar ends. Trim each onion half and remove some of the inner layers from each, creating a well in the center.
2. Mix the parsley, prosciutto, feta, and egg to form a uniform mixture. Adjust seasoning with salt and pepper.
3. Add portions of the cheese filling to the hollows of the onion halves. Rub olive oil on a baking dish and arrange the stuffed onions in the dish.
4. Drizzle some olive oil over the onions and bake at 350 degrees F for 20 minutes, or until the onions are tender and the cheese filling has browned.

Notes: Other cheeses such as dry ricotta (ricotta *salata*) or Gruyère would be a reasonable substitute. If fresh *brocciu* is available, certainly use it.

Potatoes in Ragout

POMMES DE TERRE EN RAGOÛT

TIANU DI PATATE

SERVES 6 TO 8

Potatoes are a staple of the Corsican diet. They can be found in meat and game dishes, and are often included in stews. Here, they are featured as a side dish, to accompany roasted meats or poultry.

Advance Preparation: Prepare each ingredient as directed in ingredients list.

1. Heat the oil in a heavy skillet. Add the pork and sauté over medium heat until golden, about 2 minutes.
2. Add the onion and garlic and sauté until the onion is translucent and the garlic is aromatic. Add the tomatoes and cook until they soften and begin to release their juice.
3. Add the potatoes, thyme, bay leaves, and cloves. Add enough water to come halfway up the potatoes. Add the sugar.
4. Cook over low heat until the potatoes are fork-tender, about 8 minutes, adding water as necessary.
5. Adjust seasoning with salt and pepper. Serve warm.

Notes: Prosciutto or other ham can substitute for the smoked pork loin. A grating of aged cheese would be a nice touch to finish the dish.

✳ Ingredients

¼ cup olive oil

2 ounces smoked pork loin, diced

1 medium onion, diced

2 garlic cloves, minced

2 Roma tomatoes, quartered

8 medium new potatoes, cut into large pieces

1 sprig fresh thyme

2 bay leaves

2 cloves

pinch sugar

salt and pepper

Ragout of White Beans and Leeks

Ingredients

12 ounces dried white beans, such as great northern

3 medium leeks, white and light green parts only

3 tablespoons pork fat, chicken fat, or olive oil

1 ounce pancetta or bacon, chopped

1 bay leaf

2 tablespoons chopped tomatoes

salt and pepper

RAGOÛT DE HARICOTS BLANC ET DE POIREAUX
U TIANU DI FASGIOLI E DI PORRI

SERVES 6

Beans are a valuable source of protein and can be grown in mountainous terrain, perfect for Corsican cuisine. Beans form the foundation of many soups and stews, and are also served alone or as a side dish.

Advance Preparation: Rinse the beans under running water and then soak them in salted water for 1 hour. Rinse thoroughly. Thoroughly wash the leeks and slice.

1. Heat the fat or oil in a casserole dish or deep skillet. Add the leeks and sauté 2 minutes over low heat. Add the pancetta and continue to cook 1 minute.
2. Add the soaked beans, bay leaf, and chopped tomatoes. Add enough water to cover the beans by 1-inch.
3. Cover the pan and simmer over low heat 1 hour, or until the beans are tender but have not broken down. Adjust seasoning with salt and pepper. Serve warm.

Notes: Canned beans also work well in this recipe and save time. Always rinse canned beans thoroughly under cold water before using. Skip the 1 hour soak and reduce cooking time to 15 minutes.

Fava Beans in Casserole with Dandelions

FÈVES FRAÎCHES EN COCOTTE AU PISSENLIT

FAVE FRESCHE IN ANTIBU INCU DI RADICHJU

SERVES 4

Fava beans are tolerant of cooler temperatures and can easily be cultivated in the higher altitudes of mountainous Corsica. They are prepared across North Africa and throughout the Mediterranean. Please note that there can be a serious food allergy associated with fava beans, most often with people of Mediterranean descent.

Advance Preparation: Hull the fava beans. Heat the oven to 375 degrees F.

1. In a heavy ovenproof casserole, sauté the pancetta in the olive oil over medium heat until soft but not browned. Add the onion and sauté 1 minute.
2. Stir in the hulled fava beans and sauté 1 minute. Add enough water to just cover the beans and add the salt, pepper, mint, and dandelion leaves.
3. Place the casserole, uncovered, in the oven at 375 degrees F for 30 minutes or until the water has evaporated and the bean mixture is bubbling.
4. Remove the casserole from the oven and immediately stir in the beaten egg. Serve warm.

Notes: Canned fava beans work well in this dish. Rinse them thoroughly under running water before using. Do not cover the beans with water but just have it come halfway up. Also reduce the cooking time if using canned beans. Frozen fava beans may be treated as fresh in this recipe.

Ingredients

- 2 cups fresh, tender fava beans (broad beans)
- 2 ounces pancetta or fatty bacon, diced
- 3 tablespoons olive oil
- 1 medium onion, diced
- salt and pepper
- 6 fresh mint leaves, thinly sliced
- 12 dandelion leaves, thinly sliced
- 1 egg, beaten

Rice with Olives

Ingredients

½ cup olive oil

1 small onion, diced

2 garlic cloves, minced

8 ounces pitted green olives

4 ounces dry smoked sausage (*see Notes*), sliced into medallions

9 ounces (about 1⅓ cups) long grain rice

salt and freshly ground pepper

RAGOÛT DE RIZ AUX OLIVES
U TIANU DI RISU INCU D'ULIVO

SERVES 4 TO 6

In Corsican "*tianu*" is both a stew and the glazed earthenware pot used to cook the stew. This vessel is present in most Corsican kitchens and is indispensable when preparing traditional dishes. A heavy casserole dish or crock pot will work fine to prepare this side dish.

Advance Preparation: Prepare each ingredient as directed in the ingredients list. Bring 4 cups of water to a boil for cooking the rice.

1. Heat the oil in a heavy casserole or Dutch oven. Add the onions and sauté until translucent but not browned. Stir in the garlic and cook until aromatic, about 1 minute.
2. Stir in the olives and sausage and sauté 2 minutes. Add the rice and stir until the grains are translucent and have absorbed the oil.
3. Add the 4 cups boiling water and lower the heat to a simmer. Cook undisturbed for 30 minutes, or until rice is tender, adding water if necessary.
4. Gently stir the contents and adjust seasoning with salt and pepper just before serving.

Notes: *Figatellu* is a dry, smoked liver sausage called for in this Corsican recipe. If not available, try a dry Chinese liver sausage available in Asian markets; but any lightly smoked dry-style sausage will do for this dish, including Spanish chorizo.

Corsican desserts are rustic in nature. They are not based on delicate pastry or rich creams or custards. *Brocciu*, Corsica's ubiquitous cheese, is often incorporated into its most traditional pastries. *Brocciu* makes a delicious sweet cheese filling for turnovers and small tarts, often baked during secular and religious festivals. *Fiadone* is the Corsican cheesecake enjoyed across the island that when baked with a bottom crust becomes *Tarte au Brocciu*. Fritters and beignets are also common to the home kitchen and local bakery. Chestnut flour is often used along with wheat flour to add a Corsican signature to the dough. *Panzarotti* are sweet fritters with cooked rice added to a light batter. Cakes are often yeast-raised and flavored with local liqueurs and can also have a portion of the wheat flour replaced by chestnut flour.

Confitures (preserves) and jellies are also very popular as they are a perfect way to store an ample harvest from the garden. Locally grown fruits, such as oranges, lemons, figs, citrons (*cedràt*), and the fruit of the arburtus tree (*arbouses*), are made into jams and jellies, as are tomatoes, both green and red. Chestnuts are also preserved and myrtle berries are used to make myrtle jelly. *Ratafias* (infused flavored waters and liqueurs) are also made from local fruits and herbs, and are produced in many home kitchens.

Baking is associated with holidays and festivals around the world. Corsican specialties abound, many of which celebrate Easter. *Campanille* and *caccavellu* are Easter cakes with symbolic eggs pressed into the dough before baking. On Good Friday, crisp sugarcoated cookies called *fougassi* are found in every bakery in Bonafacio. To celebrate the shearing of the sheep in late spring, turnovers filled with cheese and orange peel are baked in Sartenaise. Anise-flavored, yeast-risen doughnuts called *mighechu* signal the beginning of the Patronal Festival in Rusio in September.

DESERTS

Corsican Cheesecake

Sweet Cheese-Filled Turnovers

Wildflower Honey Cake

Sweet Brioche

Chestnut Beignets

Rice Fritters

Anise Biscuits

Almond and Chestnut Tart

Chestnut Flan with Caramel

Green Tomato Preserves

Corsican Cheesecake

Ingredients

1½ pounds whole milk ricotta

6 ounces fresh goat cheese (*chèvre*)

6 eggs

1 cup sugar

grated zest of 1 lemon

1 tablespoon myrtle liqueur or eau-de-vie

butter or oil to grease baking dish

GATEAU AU FROMAGE
FIADONE

SERVES 8 TO 12

> This dessert is a specialty of Corte, but is found throughout the island in many variations. It is the most popular dessert in Corsica. It includes brocciu, the famous cheese of this region, in its fresh form.

Advance Preparation: Stir the ricotta and place it in a coffee-filter-lined strainer or coffee drip funnel. Cover with additional filter paper and place a weight on top (a large can from the pantry works well). Place this over a container to catch the whey and refrigerate several hours. Heat the oven to 350 degrees F. Grease a 9-inch tart pan with removable bottom.

1. In a large bowl, whisk the drained ricotta with the goat cheese to form a smooth mixture. Stir in the eggs, one at a time.
2. Add the sugar, lemon zest, and liqueur and stir to combine. Pour this mixture into prepared tart pan. Bake at 350 degrees F for 45 minutes, or until browned and set in the center.
3. Allow to cool before serving. Refrigerate any leftovers.

Notes: To make it easier to remove the baked cheesecake from the pan, first line it with buttered parchment paper that is trimmed to fit. A springform pan can substitute for the tart pan to aid in removal. A common variation of this recipe is to add a bottom crust of pastry, making *Tarte au Brocciu*. Use your favorite pie dough recipe, or *pâté brisée* for a more moisture-resistant crust (see page 42).

Perched on a mountainside, with huge granite peaks in the background, mystical Corte is the seat of Corsican nationalism. It was here that Corsica's first national constitution was written in 1731 and this is the place where Pasquale Paoli formed its first democratic government. Due to its impenetrable nature, Corte was the important Corsican inland military stronghold in its fight for independence. Today, Corte is home to Corsica's only university and houses its premier museum, the *Museu di a Corsica*.

Museu di a Corsica

Sweet Cheese-Filled Turnovers

CHAUSSONS DE BROCCIU
E BASTELLE INCU U BRUCCIU

SERVES 12

> The turnovers in this recipe are shaped like little slippers or ballet shoes (*chaussons* in French) and are quite popular bakery items. If fresh brocciu is available, feel free to substitute for the ricotta and *chèvre*.

Advance Preparation: Prepare the pâté brisée a day ahead if possible, or allow for a minimum of 2 hours rest in the refrigerator. Stir the ricotta and place it in a coffee-filter-lined strainer or coffee drip funnel. Cover with additional filter paper and place a weight on top (a large can from the pantry works well). Place this over a container to catch the whey and refrigerate several hours.

1. Divide the pâté brisée and form into 12 balls. Flatten each and roll out to form circles about 4-inches in diameter.
2. Combine the drained ricotta with the goat cheese, sugar, liqueur, and salt to form a smooth mixture.
3. Add portions of cheese filling to the lower third of each pastry circle. Brush the edges with water or egg wash. Fold over and crimp around the border, forming a tight seal with no air gaps between the filling and the pastry.
4. Heat the frying oil to 365 degrees F. Deep fry the pastries, a few at a time, until golden brown and crisp. Using a slotted spoon, remove the cooked pastries to drain on paper towels. Allow to cool several minutes.
5. Dust turnovers generously with powdered sugar before serving.

Notes: The pastries may be baked at 400 degrees F for 10 to 12 minutes rather than fried. If baked, apply an egg wash to the pastries before baking.

Ingredients

- 1 recipe pâté brisée (*see recipe Spinach and Leek Tart, page 42*)
- 12 ounces whole milk ricotta
- 2 ounces fresh goat cheese (*chèvre*)
- ¼ cup sugar
- 1 tablespoon myrtle liqueur (or other liqueur such as orange or raspberry)
- pinch salt
- oil for deep frying
- powdered sugar for dusting

Wildflower Honey Cake

Ingredients

½ cup mild olive oil, safflower oil, or peanut oil

1 cup sugar

4 eggs, beaten

1 cup wildflower honey (*see Notes*)

2½ cups flour

1 tablespoon baking powder

1 teaspoon baking soda

1 teaspoon ground allspice

½ teaspoon ground cinnamon

pinch salt

1 cup orange juice

1 cup chopped roasted chestnuts (*optional*)

GÂTEAU AU MIEL DE FLEUR SAUVAGE
PASTADOLCE INCU DI MELE DI FIORE SALVATICU

Corsican honey can be mild and floral, rich and golden, or dark and brooding, depending upon the season and the fields in which the honey bees forage. For this cake a medium-bodied wildflower honey works best.

Advance Preparation: Heat the oven to 350 degrees F. Grease a 9-inch loaf pan.

1. In a large bowl, beat the oil with the sugar for 1 minute. Whisk in the eggs, one at a time. Stir in the honey.

2. Sift together the flour, baking powder, baking soda, allspice, cinnamon, and salt.

3. Add the dry ingredients to the egg mixture in portions, alternating with the orange juice, gently combining to form a smooth batter.

4. If using chestnuts, toss them with some flour to coat before folding them into the batter.

5. Pour the batter into the prepared loaf pan and bake 1 hour or until the center of the cake springs back when touched (or a wooden skewer comes out clean from the center). Allow to cool before serving.

Notes: Feel free to use any honey you like. Remember that pronounced flavors work best in baked goods. Sage blossom, clover blossom, or orange blossom honey would be excellent choices.

Sweet Brioche

PAIN DE MORTS
L'UGA SICCATA

This raisin-and-nut-filled brioche is traditionally prepared in Bonifacio on November 2, the Day of the Dead. The bread is left by visitors to cemeteries, as food for the trip to eternity for those who have passed away. Due to the demand by tourists and visitors to the region, the bread is now baked for breakfast every day.

Advance Preparation: Heat the oven to 400 degrees F about 1 hour before baking.

1. Add some hot water to a large bowl to warm it. Pour this out and add the 2 cups warm water (105 degrees F). Sprinkle the yeast over the surface and allow to stand 2 minutes in a warm place. Stir to combine.

2. Add half of the flour to the yeast mixture and stir to form a smooth mixture. Allow to stand 5 minutes in a warm place.

3. Continue to stir in flour until the mixture is sticky (but does not form a ball). Beat in the sugar, butter, and eggs, one at a time. Add the lemon zest and salt and stir to combine.

4. Continue to add flour to form a dough that cleans the sides of the bowl.

5. Toss the raisins and nuts with some flour and fold them into the dough. Cover the bowl with a damp cloth and set it in a warm place to rise for 1 hour.

6. Punch down the dough and form it into a flattened ball. Place the dough onto a baking sheet and allow the dough to rise 1 hour in a draft-free place.

7. Beat the egg yolk with an equal amount of water and brush the surface of the bread with this egg wash. Bake at 400 degrees F for 30 minutes or until the bread is thoroughly baked, golden brown, and sounds hollow when tapped. Allow to cool on a wire rack.

Notes: An electric mixer makes easy work of forming the dough. Use a paddle to mix the dough until it is sticky, but does not form a ball. Switch to a dough hook and continue to add flour until the dough cleans the sides of the bowl.

Ingredients

2 cups warm water (105 degrees F)

2 tablespoons dry yeast

4 to 5 cups all-purpose flour

½ cup sugar

4 ounces (8 tablespoons) butter, softened

2 eggs

grated zest of 1 lemon

pinch salt

12 ounces (about 2 cups) raisins

12 ounces coarsely chopped walnuts

1 egg yolk for brushing

Chestnut Beignets

Ingredients

4 cups chestnut flour

1 cup all-purpose flour (*see Notes*)

1 tablespoon dry yeast

3 tablespoons sugar

1 teaspoon vanilla extract

1¼ cups warm water

oil to fry beignets

granulated sugar to dust beignets

Beignets, or fritters, are very popular as savories with herbs and brocciu included in the batter, and as sweet treats, with a sugar dusting to finish them. Chestnut beignets can be either savory or sweet in Corsica, and here is a delightful recipe for the dessert type.

Advance Preparation: Prepare a frying area and put the oil in a deep pan or fryer.

1. Sift the flours with the yeast and sugar.

2. Add the vanilla to the water. Stir the vanilla water into the flour mixture until it forms a smooth batter. Allow to stand 2 hours. (Any lumps will dissolve upon standing. The batter should be very thick.)

3. Heat the oil to 365 degrees F. Gently drop spoonfuls of batter into the hot oil and fry, in batches, until golden and crisp. Do not crowd the fryer.

4. Remove the fried beignets to paper towels. Allow the oil to come back to desired temperature before adding the next batch.

5. Dust the beignets with granulated sugar and serve.

Notes: The addition of wheat flour to the chestnut flour produces a lighter, richer beignet. Other recipes from the island use just chestnut flour and you should try these fritters that way for a more rustic version. Chestnut flour is available through Internet retailers, and the Pacific Northwest of the U.S. is known for its fine, organically grown chestnuts.

Castagniccia, on the eastern side of the island, takes its name from the Corsican word for chestnut, *castagna*. Chestnuts were first introduced to Corsica by the Genoese in the fifteenth century and this region soon became the most populated on the island due to a highly profitable trade in chestnut flour and the wood itself. Today many of the hamlets and villages are deserted. Compared to most regions in central Corsica, Castagniccia has the most roads, albeit extremely narrow and twisting. They are still full of hazards like meandering pigs and wandering goats. The oldest fair in Corsica is the *Fiera di a Castagna* and the aroma of roasting chestnuts wafting through the air at this festival is unforgettable. The fair is held in December in Bocognano on the road between Corte and Ajaccio.

Chestnuts

Rice Fritters

BEIGNETS DE RIZ
PANZAROTTI

SERVES 6

> This recipe is from Bastia, in the north. It is said that these fritters were made long ago to celebrate the good works of Saint Joseph. Ingredients may vary from household to household, but all *panzarotti* are delicate, sweet rice fritters. This recipe is an excellent way to use leftover cooked rice.

Advance Preparation: If cooked rice is not on hand, cook ½ cup raw rice with sufficient water until just tender, about 10 minutes. Drain and cool.

1. Add some hot water to a large bowl to warm it and then pour it out. Add the 1½ cups warm water and sprinkle the yeast over the surface. Allow it to stand 2 minutes. Stir to incorporate.
2. Whisk half of the flour into the yeast mixture and allow to stand 5 minutes.
3. Stir in the egg yolks, myrtle liqueur, olive oil, and lemon zest.
4. Add the remaining flour and powdered sugar and stir to form a smooth batter.
5. Add the cooked rice and gently mix to incorporate.
6. Beat the egg whites to form soft peaks and gently fold them into the batter. Allow batter to stand 1 hour before using.
7. Heat the oil for frying to 370 degrees F. Drop spoonfuls of batter into the oil and cook until golden, about 3 minutes. Remove the cooked fritters to drain on paper towels.
8. Dust the fritters with powdered sugar before serving.

Notes: In Centuri (in Cap Corse), *panzarotti* are stuffed with a sweet filling of raisins and chard. Rather than a batter, the pastry is firm and rolled out. The filling is incorporated and the assemblage is cut into pieces and fried.

Ingredients

1½ cups warm water

1 tablespoon dry yeast

2⅔ cups all-purpose flour

4 eggs, separated

½ cup myrtle liqueur or eau-de-vie

2 tablespoons light olive oil

grated zest of 1 lemon

¼ cup powdered sugar

1½ cups cooked rice (*see Advance Preparation*)

oil for frying

powdered sugar for dusting

Anise Biscuits

Ingredients

1 tablespoon dry yeast

¼ cup warm water

¾ cup (12 tablespoons) butter, softened

¾ cup sugar

¼ cup dry white wine

¼ cup anise flavored liqueur, such as pastis

4½ cups all-purpose flour

pinch salt

These dry biscuits, flavored with anise, may remind you of Italian biscotti, in that they are very dry and crisp and can be stored for long periods without spoiling. Corsicans make these in large batches so there are always some handy for a drop-in visitor to enjoy.

Advance Preparation: Dissolve the yeast into ¼ cup of warm water. Allow to stand 3 minutes.

1. Cream the butter and sugar together until light and fluffy. Stir in the wine and anise liqueur. Add the dissolved yeast and mix thoroughly.
2. Add the flour and salt and stir to combine and form a soft dough that is not sticky and can be rolled out. A bit more flour or water may be needed.
3. Roll the dough out to a thickness of ½-inch. Cut into squares, rectangles, or diamonds about 2-inches in size. Place on parchment-lined baking or cookie sheet pans. Do not crowd them. Loosely cover the pans with plastic wrap and allow to rest 1 hour before baking.
4. Heat the oven to 325 degress F. Bake the biscuits for about 1 hour, or until the biscuits are dry and crisp.
5. Allow the biscuits to cool on wire racks. Store in tightly sealed containers in a cool, dry place.

Notes: Consider this recipe a base from which to add a variety of ingredients, as is done across Corsica. Some tasty additions include raisins, toasted almonds, and lemon or orange zest. Some of the liquid may be replaced by eggs, and the softened butter may be replaced by a light flavored oil, such as peanut or safflower. The anise liqueur may be replaced by additional wine, should the licorice-like taste of anise not appeal to you.

Almond and Chestnut Tart

TARTE FONDANTE AUX CHÂTAIGNES
TORTA FUNDENTE INCU DI CASTAGNE

Chestnuts can be purchased in a variety of forms. In addition to fresh and dried chestnuts, *marrons glacés*, candied chestnuts, and chestnut purée, called for in this recipe, can be found in gourmet markets.

Advance Preparation: To make your own chestnut purée, cook 12 ounces fresh chestnuts that have been peeled in enough milk to cover for 30 minutes. Drain and pass the cooked chestnuts through a food mill or purée in a food processor. Allow to cool before using. Grease a 9-inch removable-bottom tart pan.

1. In a large bowl, mix the flours together and stir in the melted butter, egg yolk, and sugar. Gently knead to form a smooth dough. If too dry add some cold water; if too sticky add a bit of flour. Wrap in plastic wrap and allow to rest 1 hour.

2. Heat the oven to 375 degrees F. Mix the chestnut purée with the honey, 2 eggs, cream, and almonds.

3. Roll the pastry out and use to line the greased tart pan. Prick the surface with a fork to prevent puffing when baked blind. Bake the pastry for 10 minutes or until just set and not well browned.

4. Pour the chestnut filling into the crust and bake an additional 20 minutes or until golden brown and set in the center. Cool on a wire rack before serving.

Notes: If using dried chestnuts for the purée, rinse them thoroughly and then cover with water in a medium pan. Simmer 10 minutes over low heat. Remove the pan from the heat and cover. Allow to stand 1 hour and then drain. Use as directed for fresh.

❈ Ingredients

1 cup chestnut flour

1 cup all-purpose flour

4 ounces (8 tablespoons) butter, melted

1 egg yolk

¼ cup sugar

1½ cups chestnut purée, store-bought or homemade (*see Advance Preparation*)

⅓ cup honey, preferably wildflower or chestnut honey, if available

2 eggs

½ cup cream

4 ounces chopped skinless almonds, toasted

Chestnut Flan with Caramel

Ingredients

3 tablespoons chestnut flour

2 tablespoons all-purpose flour

1 quart whole milk

1 cup sugar

1 teaspoon pure vanilla extract

6 eggs

FLAN AU LAIT ET CHÂTAIGNES AU CARAMEL
PASTIZZU DI CASTAGNE AU CARAMELLU

SERVES 4 TO 6

Baked custards are enjoyed around the world and Corsica is no exception. The Corsican pantry is always stocked with eggs, which are often used to enrich a basic dinner meal.

Advance Preparation: Heat the oven to 325 degrees F.

1. In a large saucepan, mix the flours with just enough milk to form a smooth, thin paste.
2. Whisk the remaining milk into flour paste along with ¾ cup of the sugar and the vanilla. Cook over low heat 10 minutes, or until the mixture is simmering and there is no raw flour taste.
3. Remove the milk mixture from the heat and allow to cool.
4. In a small heavy pan, heat the remaining ¼ cup sugar to a light caramel, being careful not to burn the sugar. The addition of a few tablespoons of water to the sugar can slow down the process.
5. Pour the caramel into the bottom of a 2-quart baking pan, rotating the pan quickly to evenly coat the bottom of the pan.
6. Whisk the eggs into the cooled milk mixture and pour this into the caramel-coated pan. Bake at 325 degress F for 40 minutes, or until set and a knife point comes out clean from the center of the custard.
7. Allow to cool before inverting the flan onto a serving dish large enough to catch any runoff of caramel sauce from the baking pan.

Notes: The addition of ¼ cup of chestnut purée would add nicely to the flavor. Stir this in with the eggs, just before baking.

Green Tomato Preserves

CONFITURE DE TOMATES VERTES

U CUNFITURA DI PUMMATA VERDI

Ingredients

3 pounds green tomatoes

2 lemons, peeled, with all white pith removed

2¼ pounds sugar

> Preserves, as their name implies, are an excellent way to store delicate fruits over long periods. The technique of making preserves and jams originated with the Arabs, who also introduced sugar to the Europeans. On Corsica, preserves are made from chestnuts, figs, oranges, tomatoes, citron, lemons, and the fruit of the arbutus tree, to name just a few.

Advance Preparation: This recipe takes 2 days to prepare.

1. Drop the tomatoes into boiling water for about 1 minute, until the skins loosen. Drop them into ice water and then peel. Cut the tomatoes into quarters and remove the seeds.
2. Slice the lemons into rounds. Remove the seeds.
3. Layer portions of tomatoes, sugar, and lemon slices, in that order, in a non-reactive casserole dish (usable on stovetop) until all are used. Allow to stand at room temperature, covered, overnight.
4. The next day place the casserole over medium heat and bring the contents to a boil. Lower the heat and simmer 30 minutes. Reduce the heat and slowly cook for 1 hour. The preserves are ready when a small amount of the cooking liquid does not spread when dropped onto a plate.
5. Store the preserves in the refrigerator in clean, sealed jars.

Notes: Other fruits can be preserved in this way. A rule of thumb is to use roughly equal amounts (by weight) of fruit and sugar, adjusting for the inherent sweetness of the fruit used.

Glossary of Corsican Foods

Aziminu A Corsican version of bouillabaisse.

Bastelicacciu A creamy sheep's milk cheese from Bastelica.

Brocciu Corsica's "national" cheese, made from goat's milk and/or sheep's milk, ranging in texture from soft (like cream cheese or ricotta) to grating firmness (like parmesan), depending upon age.

Bugliticca A cheese beignet made from goat's or sheep's milk, originating in Castagniccia.

Caccavellu A brioche bread baked for the Easter season, often incorporating unshelled eggs on top.

Calinzana A piquant, fresh sheep's or goat's milk cheese without rind from Calenzana.

Campanile A traditional crown-shaped pastry baked during Easter, with unshelled eggs pressed in the dough before baking.

Canestra A brioche pastry, crown shaped, brown and crisp outside, soft and rich inside.

Canistrellu A crisp biscuit, long and cylindrical, made with white wine and oil.

Castagnacciu A rich, moist cake made with chestnut flour from Bastia.

Chjerchjole Baked miniature goat cheese cakes on chestnut leaves from Calenzana.

Coppa Pork loin that has been salted, smoked, and then hung in caves to dry and age.

The *Festa di a Brocciu* is held in May in the lovely village of Piana, just a few kilometers south of Porto in the northwestern section of Corsica. The spectacular red rock formations called the Calanches form a breathtaking backdrop to the village and are popular among rock climbers. Brocciu, Corsica's most ubiquitous ingredient, is a cheese of many characters. It can be made from ewe's milk, goat's milk, or a mixture of the two. When fresh it may remind you of a tangy ricotta. As it ages and dries it can be crumbled, eventually becoming a fine grating cheese like parmesan. Brocciu became a recognized regional cheese of France in 1983 when it was granted an Appellation of Origin (AOC) by the government.

Brocciu

Curcones Small yeast-raised cakes, rolled in sugar, served during the Easter season.

Cuscio A raw sheep's milk cheese from the valley of Tavaro, often prepared with myrtle wood paddles to add flavor.

Falculella A galette made with brocciu and dried chestnuts, a specialty of Corte in Haute-Corse; also sweet pastry turnovers, filled with brocciu, popular in Vico.

Fenuchjettu A long biscuit with visible anise seeds from Ajaccio.

Fiadone The famous cheesecake of Corsica, made with brocciu and flavored with myrtle liqueur and enjoyed in all regions.

Figatellu A sausage made from pork liver, lean meat, various organs, and blood, seasoned with laurel, rosemary, garlic, and red wine.

Fougassi Thin round cookies, flavored with *pastis*, glazed with sugar, served on Good Friday in Bonifacio.

Fritelli Fried beignets, filled with brocciu, dusted with sugar, popularized in Porto-Veccio and served everywhere.

Imbrucciata A small cheese tartlet, popular in the south, in the region surrounding Ajaccio.

Imbrucciate A cheesecake made with brocciu (*see Fiadone*), in a puff pastry crust.

Lonzu Loin of pork that has been salted and dried, and coated with cracked pepper.

Maccaredda Small, savory chestnut cakes made with salt pork.

Mighechu Yeast-raised sweetened bread balls, flavored with *pastis*, served during the Patronal Festival in Rusio on September 8.

Migliacci Small yeast-raised cakes or a large cheese galette, served on a bed of chestnut leaves, typical of northern Corsica.

Misgiscia Dried, salted strips of goat meat that have been first marinated in vinegar.

Nicci Twice-baked chestnut biscuits, baked on fresh chestnut leaves.

Panzarottu Rice fritters from Bastia, served on St.Joseph's Day; they are also found in Ajaccio filled with chard.

Panzetta A roll of lean bacon made from the breast of pork, known as pancetta in Italy.

Pestu A salt cod dish, prepared with tomatoes, nuts, and anchovies.

Prisuttu Air-dried and cave-cured ham, similar to prosciutto or Bayonne ham.

Razighes Savory yeast raised dumplings with pork cracklings left over from making lard.

Rivia A mixed plate of roasted shoulder of baby goat, served with grilled intestines and other organs, from Porto-Veccio.

Salamu An air-dried salami made from pork or boar.

Sangui Blood sausage made with chard, onions, and/or raisins.

Sciacci Round sweet cheese turnovers, flavored with dried orange peel, from Sartenaise, served during the time of shearing of the sheep, in May, traditionally baked on granite; also baked pastries filled with potatoes, traditionally served on All Saints' Day in Levie.

Storzapreti Quenelles of cheese and chard, served alone or to accompany meats in sauce.

Strenna Similar to *sciacci*, but in Vico it is baked as a large tart with a top crust and served on New Year's Day.

Stufatu A meat or vegetable stew usually including pasta or cooked cornmeal.

Venacu A goat's or sheep's milk cheese with an orange rind, from Venaco in the central region.

Ventra Stuffed pig stomach with chard and onions, served on Christmas day.

Corsican-English Culinary Terms

abbrustuli – grilled
acetu – vinegar
afumicà – smoked
agliu – garlic
agnellu – lamb
alivi – olives
alloru – bay laurel
anatra – duck
anchjovi – anchovy
anguilla – eel
aranciu – orange
arrustiti – rotisserie
artichjocci – artichokes
arusita – grilled
baccala – cod
bastelle – turnover
biscottu – biscuit
boie – beef
brodu – broth, bouillon
buliati – boiled
camisgia – poached
camumilla – chamomile
capra – goat, chèvre
caprettu – kid goat
caprunu – goat
caramellu – caramel
carbusgiu – cabbage; green cabbage
carne – meat
casgiu – cheese
castagne – chestnuts
castagnigna – chestnut flour
caulifiore – cauliflower
ceci – chickpeas
cee – Swiss chard
chjarasgi – cherries
civolle – onion
colombi – pigeon
cunigliulu – rabbit
curata – innards
cusciottu – leg of
dolci – sweet
erba – herb
erba barona – thyme
farina – flour

farin di granonu – cornmeal
farzitu – stuffed
fasgianu – pheasant
fasgiolu – beans
fave fresche – broadbeans
fecatu – liver
ficci – figs
filettu – tenderloin
finóchju – fennel
fornu – baked
freschi – fresh
fritelle – beignet
frittata – omelet
fritte – fried
fungi – mushrooms
ghjamba – leg of
granci – crab(s)
lardu – bacon
lentichje – lentils
lumache – snails
lupacante – lobster
maiale – pork
marinata – marinated
mele – honey
melzana – eggplant
menta – mint
minestra – soup
mirizani – eggplant
mollu – marinade
morta – myrtle
muscule – mussels
olive – olive
ove – egg
pane – bread
parmici – pigeon
pasizzu – gratin
pastizzu – pâté
patata – potato
peveroni – bell pepper
picurinu – lamb
pieni – stuffed
piselli – peas
pisi – green peas
polpu – octopus

porri – leeks
presche – peach
puddestru – chicken
pulenda – polenta
pullastru – chicken
pullastru di cornovagliu – Cornish
    game hen
pulpetta – dumplings (quenelles)
pummata – tomato
purcelluciu – suckling pig
quagliu – quail
radichju – dandelion
risu – rice
rossi – red
rumu – rum
salsa – sauce
salvaticu – wild
salvia – sage
sardine – sardines
sdruttu – bacon
seccu – dried
singhjari – wild boar
spalla – shoulder of
spinaciu – spinach
suffaitu – soufflé
taglia – sliced
tappane – capers
tianu – stew
timu – thyme
tonnu – tuna
torta – tart
totanu – calamari (squid)
trippa – tripe
truite – trout
usciatu – flamed
uva – grape
uva secca – raisins
verdi – green
vinu – wine
vitellu – veal
zinu – sea urchin
zucca – squash
zuchine – zucchini

English-Corsican Culinary Terms

anchovy – *anchjovi*
artichokes – *artichjocci*
bacon – *lardu*; *sdruttu*
baked – *fornu*
bay laurel – *alloru*
beans – *fasgiolu*
beef – *boie*
beignet – *fritelle*
bell pepper – *peveroni*
biscuit – *biscottu*
boiled – *buliati*
bread – *pane*
broadbeans – *fave fresche*
broth – *brodu*
cabbage – *carbusgiu*
calamari (squid) – *totanu*
capers – *tappane*
caramel – *caramellu*
cauliflower – *caulifiore*
chamomile – *camumilla*
cheese – *casgiu*
cherries – *chjarasgi*
chestnut flour – *castagnigna*
chestnuts – *castagne*
chicken – *pullastru*; *puddestru*
chickpeas – *ceci*
cod – *baccala*
Cornish game hen – *pullastru di cornovagliu*
cornmeal – *farin di granonu*
crab(s) – *granci*
dandelion – *radichju*
dried – *seccu*
duck – *anatra*
dumplings (quenelles) – *pulpetta*
eel – *anguilla*
egg – *ove*
eggplant – *melzana*; *mirizani*
fennel – *finóchju*
figs – *ficci*
flamed – *usciatu*

flour – *farina*
fresh – *freschi*
fried – *fritte*
garlic – *agliu*
goat – *capra*; *caprunu*
grape – *uva*
gratin – *pasizzu*
green – *verdi*
green cabbage – *carbusgiu*
green peas – *pisi*
grilled – *arusita*; *abbrustuli*
herb – *erba*
honey – *mele*
innards – *curata*
kid goat – *caprettu*
lamb – *agnellu*; *picurinu*
leeks – *porri*
leg of – *ghjamba*; *cusciottu*
lentils – *lentichje*
liver – *fecatu*
lobster – *lupacante*
marinade – *mollu*
marinated – *marinata*
meat – *carne*
mint – *menta*
mushrooms – *fungi*
mussels – *muscule*
myrtle – *morta*; *mortula*
octopus – *polpu*
olive – *olive*
omelet – *frittata*
onion – *civolle*
orange – *aranciu*
pâté – *pastizzu*
peach – *presche*
peas – *piselli*
pheasant – *fasgianu*
pigeon – *colombi*; *parmici*
poached – *camisgia*
polenta – *pulenda*
pork – *maiale*

potato – *patata*
quail – *quagliu*
rabbit – *cunigliulu*
raisins – *uva secca*
red – *rossi*
rice – *risu*
rotisserie – *arrustiti*
rum – *rumu*
sage – *salvia*
sardines – *sardine*
sauce – *salsa*
sea urchin – *zinu*
shoulder of – *spalla*
sliced – *taglia*
smoked – *afumicà*
snails – *lumache*
soufflé – *suffaitu*
soup – *minestra*
spinach – *spinaciu*
squash – *zucca*
stew – *tianu*
stuffed – *farzitu*; *pieni*
suckling pig – *purcelluciu*
sweet – *dolci*
Swiss chard – *cee*
tart – *torta*
tenderloin – *filettu*
thyme – *erba barona*; *timu*
tomato – *pummata*
tripe – *trippa*
trout – *truite*
tuna – *tonnu*
turnover – *bastelle*
veal – *vitellu*
vinegar – *acetu*
wild – *salvaticu*
wild boar – *singhjari*
wine – *vinu*
zucchini – *zuchine*

CREDITS

Photography – David H. Weber
Illustrations – John A. Wilson
Food Styling and Additional Photography – Arthur L. Meyer
Tableware – Rosenthal China; Homer Laughlin

ACKNOWLEDGMENTS

Mick Vann, co-author of the *Appetizer Atlas*. Together we "discovered" Corsican cuisine while researching the book. I owe a great deal of thanks to Mick. This book would not be possible without his preliminary research and enthusiasm for the subject.

Priti Chitnis Gress and the entire staff of Hippocrene Books, Inc. for their ideas, support, and cooperation.

Maddy Thein for preserving Corsican food traditions and for her modern interpretations of the cuisine.

BIBLIOGRAPHY

_____. *Corse- Produits du terroir et recettes traditionnelles*. Paris: Èditions Albin Michel, 1996.
Costa, Edith. *Pour le Plaisir de Recevoir, La Corse*. Sommières: Romain Pages Èditions, 2005.
Fusina, Jacques. *Parlons Corse*. Paris: Èditions l'Harmattan, 1999.
Paghiola, Maud. *La Cuisine des Corses*. Nimes: Èditions Lacour, 2000.
Perrin-Chattard, Brigette et Jean-Pierre. *Mieux connaître la Cuisine Corse*. France: Èditions Gisserot, 1999.
Poli, François. *Tutta a cucina corsa*. France: Èditions du Rocher, 1983.
Ricciardi-Bartoli, F. *Cuisine de Corse de A à Z*. Paris: Èditions Bonneton, 2001.
Schapira, Christiane. *La Bonne Cuisine Corse*. Tours: Èditions Solar, 1994.
Thein, Maddy. *Cuisine Corse*. Colomars: Èditions Séquoïa, 2006.

Index

Hippocrene brings the world to your table

Cuisines of the Alps
Kay Shaw Nelson

Cuisines of the Alps takes a culinary tour through the 750-mile mountainous stretch from the Mediterranean Sea to the Balkan Peninsula, with stops in Northern Italy for *Risotto alla Milanese* and *Osso Buco*, in Austria for goulash and linzer torte, for dumplings in Bavaria, *raclette* in Switzerland, French *trout au bleu*, and in Slovenia for eggplant stew and walnut cake, among many other delights. The recipes will enhance your knowledge of the region's cookery, bringing a variety of robust, hearty dishes to your table.
0-7818-1058-2 · $24.95

Cucina di Calabria:
Treasured Recipes and Family Traditions
in Southern Italy
Mary Amabile Palmer

For centuries, Calabrian food has remained relatively undiscovered because few recipes were divulged beyond tightly-knit villages or even family circles, but Palmer has gathered a comprehensive collection of nearly 200 exciting recipes. All start with simple, fresh ingredients, transformed into sumptuous dishes with minimal effort. They are interwoven with anecdotes about Calabrian culture and history, traditions, festivals, folklore, and of course, the primary role that food plays in all aspects of Italian life. Complete with illustrations.
0-7818-1050-7 · $22.50 pb

A Ligurian Kitchen:
Recipes and Tales from the Italian Riviera
Laura Giannatempo

The Ligurian kitchen is famous for fish, fresh produce, and herbs. Dishes like *Maltagliati con Pesto Piccantino* (Fresh Maltagliati with Spicy Purple Pesto) and *Ciuppin con Crostoni di Paprika* (Ligurian Seafood Bisque with Paprika Crostoni) are featured here along with such quintessential favorites as *Tonno alla Genovese* (Seared Tuna with Porcini Ragu). But tales of lovable uncles and a lyrical account of making pasta in the midst of a storm tantalize as much as the sumptuous repasts the author places before us. In these 100 recipes and a beautiful section of photographs, the specialties of artisanal bread bakers and those of the region's *cucina povera* create a zestful collection that exemplifies "that extraordinary marriage of land and sea that is Ligurian cuisine."
0-7818-1171-6 · $29.00

My Love for Naples

Anna Teresa Callen

"[Anna Teresa Callen] is one of the national treasures of Italian cookery."
—Mario Batali, Chef, Babbo Ristorante, New York and Author, *Molto Italiano*

In this lovingly rendered cookbook memoir, readers take a culinary journey to Naples, one of the author's favorite Italian cities. From antipasti, soups, and pizza, to a host of pasta, fish, meat, and vegetable dishes, this collection of more than 250 recipes covers the cuisine of the Campania region, including its capital, Naples, the islands of Capri and Ischia, and the Amalfi coast. Neapolitan cuisine exemplifies *la cucina povera* or "the cooking of the poor", whose inventiveness with inexpensive local ingredients produced the region's legendary *mozzarella di bufala*, the famed, succulent *ragu alla napoletana*, and simple, hearty dishes that make the most of seasonal vegetables and abundant seafood. A skilled cooking instructor, the author provides easy, step-by-step instructions and much more.
978-7818-1205-4 · $35.00

Cucina Piemontese: The Cooking of Italy's Piedmont

Maria Grazia Asselle and Brian Yarvin

Cucina Piemontese includes recipes for more than 95 Piedmont dishes, many of them from the authors' family. These classic recipes, accompanied by historical and cultural information, as well as a chapter on regional wines, provide an opportunity to explore this fascinating and increasingly renowned cuisine from an insider's perspective. The simple dishes made with readily available ingredients will turn your kitchen into a *cucina piemontese*.
0-7818-1123-6 · $24.95

Pied Noir Cookbook: French Sephardic Cuisine from Algeria

Chantal Clabrough

The origins of the Jewish population in Algeria can be traced to the tenth century BCE. The Spanish Inquisition led to a growth of this community due to Jewish immigrants fleeing Europe. Later, their culture became heavily influenced by France after becoming a French colony in 1830. These recipes explore the unique heritage of Pied Noir cuisine, with dishes like Couscous with White Beans, turmeric-infused *Boeuf aux Oignons*, and *Mekroud*, or date fritters.
0-7818-1082-5 · $24.95

Cuisines of Portuguese Encounters, *Expanded Edition*
Cherie Y. Hamilton

One of the first cookbooks to encompass the entire Portuguese-speaking world is now enriched by over 70 new recipes! The expanded edition is a fascinating collection of 279 authentic recipes that illustrate how Portugal and its former colonies influenced each other's culinary traditions. From famous dishes like spicy pork *vindaloo* from Goa, the classic *bacalhau* of Portugal, and all varieties of *feijoada*, to lesser-known treats like Guinean oyster stew and coconut pudding from East Timor, this cookbook has something for every adventurous gastronome. Also includes menus for religious holidays and festive occasions, a glossary, a section on mail-order resources, and a bilingual index.
978-0-7818-1181-1 · $29.95

Sicilian Feasts
Giovanna Bellia La Marca

Sicilian Feasts was born out of the author's love for her native Sicily. She shares the history, customs, and folklore, as well as the flavorful cuisine of her beautiful Mediterranean island in recipes and anecdotes. Featuring more than 160 recipes, La Marca uses simple methods and readily available ingredients to teach the straightforward and delectable everyday cooking of Sicily, thus allowing even novices to create feasts in their kitchens. Complete with menus for holidays, notes on ingredients, a list of suppliers, an introduction to the Sicilian language, and a glossary of food terms in Sicilian, Italian, and English. Illustrations demonstrate special techniques.
0-7818-0967-3 · $24.95

Tastes from a Tuscan Kitchen
Madeline Armillotta and Diane Nocentini

Over the years, the authors have collected many recipes from friends and relatives living in the Tuscan region and throughout Italy; here, they present over 150 of the best. Here you will find a wide variety of recipes, ranging from such staples as *Pasta e Lenticchie* (Pasta and Lentils), *Cacciucco* (Fish Soup), *L'Impasto* (pizza doughs), to *Castoletti di Maiale con Salvia e Chianti* (Pork Chops with Sage and Chianti), *Scaloppine al Limone* (Veal Scallops with Lemon Sauce) and *Polpette di Macinato* (Tuscan Meatballs). Delicate crêpes are stuffed with a variety of savory fillings and covered with the perfect topping—a creamy, rich Béchamel Sauce. Then there are the sweet crêpes and charmingly named *Bongo* (Chocolate Profiteroles) that easily melt in your mouth. Tuscan sauces, crostini toppings fragrant with herbs, creamy risottos, even delightful ways to use leftovers—try *Polpette di Patate* (Italian Potato Cakes)—will have you turning again and again to this charming compilation of recipes.
0-7818-1147-3 · $24.95

Also available from Hippocrene Books

Beginner's French
0-7818-0863-4 · $16.95 pb

French-English/English-French Dictionary & Phrasebook
0-7818-0856-1 · $11.95 pb

Beginner's Italian
0-7818-0839-1 · $14.95 pb

Italian-English/English-Italian Dictionary and Phrasebook
0-7818-0812-X · $11.95 pb

Instant Italian Vocabulary Builder with CD,
Revised Edition
978-0-7818-1169-9 · $19.95 pb